W9-BEV-555

Using the Standards
Measurement

Grade 5

by
Jillayne Prince Wallaker

Published by Instructional Fair
an imprint of
Frank Schaffer Publications®

Instructional Fair

Author: Jillayne Prince Wallaker
Editor: Sara Bierling

Frank Schaffer Publications®

Instructional Fair is an imprint of Frank Schaffer Publications.

Send all inquiries to:
Frank Schaffer Publications
8720 Orion Place
Columbus, Ohio 43240

Using the Standards: Measurement—grade 5

ISBN: 0-7424-2895-8

5 6 7 8 9 10 PAT 12 11 10 09

Table of Contents

3

Introduction

This book is designed around the standards from the National Council of Teachers of Mathematics (NCTM) with a focus on measurement. Students will build new mathematical knowledge, solve problems in context, apply and adapt appropriate strategies, and reflect on processes.

The NCTM process standards are also incorporated throughout the activities. The correlation chart on page 6 identifies the pages on which each NCTM measurement substandard appears. Also look for the following process icons on each page.

 Problem Solving   Connections   Reasoning and Proof

 Communication   Representation

Workbook Pages: These activities can be done independently, in pairs, or in groups. The problems are designed to stimulate higher-level thinking skills and address a variety of learning styles.

Problems may be broken into parts, with class discussion following student work. Students may gravitate toward using these strategies, but they should also be encouraged to create and share their own strategies.

Many activities will lead into subjects that could be investigated or discussed further as a class. You may want to compare different solution methods or discuss how to select a valid solution method for a particular problem.

Communication: Most activities have a communication section. These questions may be used as journal prompts, writing activities, or discussion prompts. Each communication question is labeled **THINK** or **DO MORE**.

Create Your Own Problems: These pages prompt students to create problems like those completed on the worksheet pages. Encourage students to be creative and to use their everyday experiences. The students' responses will help you to assess their practical knowledge of the topic.

Check Your Skills: These activities provide a representative sample of the types of problems developed throughout each section. These can be used as additional practice or as assessment tools.

Reproducible Rulers: An inch ruler and a centimeter ruler are provided on page 120 for your convenience.

Vocabulary Cards: Use the vocabulary cards to familiarize students with mathematical language. The pages may be copied, cut, and pasted onto index cards. Paste the front and back on the same index card to make flash cards, or paste each side on separate cards to use in matching games or other activities.

4

Introduction (cont.)

Assessment: Assessment is an integral part of the learning process and can include observations, conversations, interviews, interactive journals, writing prompts, and independent quizzes or tests. Classroom discussions help students learn the difference between poor, good, and excellent responses. Scoring guides can help you analyze students' responses. The following is a possible list of problem-solving steps. Modify this list as necessary to fit specific problems.

1—Student understands the problem and knows what he is being asked to find.

2—Student selects an appropriate strategy or process to solve the problem.

3—Student is able to model the problem with appropriate manipulatives, graphs, tables, pictures, or computations.

4—Student is able to clearly explain or demonstrate his thinking and reasoning.

0-7424-2895-8 *Using the Standards—Measurement*

NCTM Standards Correlation Chart

		Problem Solving	Reasoning and Proof	Communication	Connections	Representation
Processes	understand attributes and select units	36, 37, 42, 43	22, 36, 37, 42, 43	9, 10, 36, 42, 43	23	9, 10, 22, 23
	standard units	11, 12-13, 25, 38, 44, 48	11, 25	12-13, 14, 25, 38, 47, 48	24, 44, 48	11, 12-13, 14, 24, 44, 47
	simple unit conversions	15, 16, 17, 18, 39, 40, 45, 46, 51, 53-54, 55	15, 46	18	15, 16, 17, 18, 39, 40, 45, 46, 49, 51, 53-54, 55	9
	precision	41, 50, 52, 56	19, 20, 21, 41, 56, 57	19, 20, 21, 26, 41, 56, 57	26, 50, 57	20, 21, 26, 50, 52
	how changing a shape affects measurement	30, 31	27, 28, 29, 30, 32, 33, 34, 35	27, 28, 29, 31, 32, 33, 34, 35	30	27, 28, 29, 32, 33, 34, 35
Techniques & Tools	estimate with irregular shapes	64, 67	67, 68, 70, 71, 72, 73, 74, 91	73	64, 67, 71	68, 70, 71, 72, 73, 74, 91
	select and apply units and tools	62, 95, 98, 100, 101, 102	62	62, 98, 101	95, 97, 98, 99, 100, 102	
	benchmarks and estimation	64, 92, 93, 94, 96	63, 92, 94, 96	63, 92, 93, 94, 96	64, 69, 103	63, 69, 93, 103
	formulas	65-66, 76, 77, 78, 79, 80	65-66, 75, 76, 77, 78	79	65-66, 75, 79, 80	75
	surface area and volume	87, 88	81, 82, 83, 85, 86, 89, 90	81, 83, 87, 88	83, 84, 85, 86, 87, 89, 90	81, 84, 86, 89, 90

The pretest, post test, Create Your Own Problems, and Check Your Skills pages are not included on this chart but contain a representative sampling of the process standards. Many pages also contain **THINK** or **DO MORE** sections, which encourage students to communicate about what they have learned.

0-7424-2895-8 *Using the Standards—Measurement*

Name _____ Date _____

Pretest

1. Hassan originally tried a 20-gram mass to make the pans balance. Pan B was lower than pan A. Next he tried this. What should he do now?

a. add more mass
b. take mass away

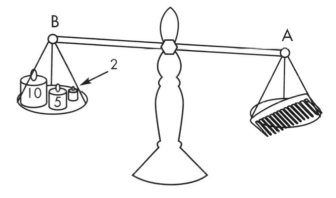

How much?

a. 2 grams
b. 5 grams
c. 10 grams
d. 20 grams

Explain your decision.

_____

_____

_____

_____

Circle the most reasonable measurement unit for each problem.

2. length of a child's hand	centimeters	meters
3. volume of a truckload of sand	cubic inches	cubic yards
4. distance from Chicago to Houston	yards	miles
5. mass of a pencil eraser	grams	kilograms
6. capacity of a car's fuel tank	milliliters	liters

Find the perimeter.

7. ⟋22⟍   _____
     11

Find the area.

8. △ 12   _____
   8

9. Marianne's filled backpack is 3.63 kilograms. Her weekly take-home binder is 1,474 grams. How many kilograms is the rest? _____

7

Pretest (cont.)

Draw an example of each angle.

10. acute angle

11. obtuse angle

12. reflex angle

13. right angle

14. straight angle

Convert each measure.

15. 4 pounds = _____ ounces

16. 41 degrees Fahrenheit = _____ degrees Celsius

17. 190 centimeters = _____ meters

18. 2 quarts = _____ fluid ounces

Find the volume and surface area of each figure.

19. volume = _____ surface area = _____

20. volume = _____ surface area = _____

19.

20.

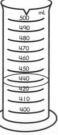

Measure each angle.

21. angle ∠BDC _____

22. angle ∠MKL _____

23. Without using a protractor, what is the measure of angle ADB? _____

What about angle JKM? _____

Find the measure.

24. _____

25. _____

0-7424-2895-8 *Using the Standards—Measurement*

Name _____ Date _____

Inching Along

Read and follow the directions. Do not list objects more than once.

1. Draw a line that is $3\frac{1}{2}$ inches long.

2. Find 3 classroom objects less than $3\frac{1}{2}$ inches long. List them here.

a. _____ b. _____ c. _____

3. Find 3 classroom objects greater than $3\frac{1}{2}$ inches long. List them here.

a. _____ b. _____ c. _____

4. Draw a line that is $7\frac{1}{4}$ inches long.

5. Find 6 classroom objects between $3\frac{1}{2}$ inches and $7\frac{1}{4}$ inches in length. List them here.

a. _____ b. _____ c. _____ d. _____ e. _____ f. _____

6. Draw a line that is $5\frac{1}{8}$ inches long.

7. Find 3 classroom objects between $3\frac{1}{2}$ and $5\frac{1}{8}$ inches in length. List them here.

a. _____ b. _____ c. _____

8. Find 3 classroom objects between $5\frac{1}{8}$ and $7\frac{1}{4}$ inches in length. List them here.

a. _____ b. _____ c. _____

DO MORE

 Measure each of the above lines to the nearest $\frac{1}{16}$ inch. Explain in writing what was difficult about this.

9

Name _____ Date _____

Collecting Centimeters

Read and follow the directions. Do not list objects more than once.

1. Draw a line that is 12 centimeters long.

2. Find 3 objects less than 12 centimeters long. List them here.

a. _____ b. _____ c. _____

3. Find 3 objects greater than 12 centimeters long. List them here.

a. _____ b. _____ c. _____

4. Draw a line that is 6 centimeters long.

5. Find 6 objects between 6 centimeters and 12 centimeters in length. List them here.

a. _____ b. _____ c. _____ d. _____ e. _____ f. _____

6. Draw a line that is 19 centimeters long.

7. Find 3 objects longer than 19 centimeters in length. List them here.

a. _____ b. _____ c. _____

8. Find 3 objects between 12 centimeters and 19 centimeters in length. List them here.

a. _____ b. _____ c. _____

DO MORE

Create a chart that shows the relationship among meters, centimeters, and millimeters.

0-7424-2895-8 *Using the Standards—Measurement*

Name _____ Date _____

Looking for the Best Answer

Read. Circle the best answer. Use a meter stick to evaluate each measurement choice.

1.	The length of Jade's new pencil is about . . .	18.5 cm	1.85 cm	185 cm
2.	Edmundo has a paper clip. Its length is about . . .	4.5 mm	45 mm	0.45 mm
3.	The height of the classroom door is about . . .	205 m	20.5 m	2.05 m
4.	George needs a new bicycle tire. Its diameter is about . . .	65 dm	6.5 dm	650 dm
5.	Abby just got a kitten. The height of the kitten is about . . .	15 cm	1.5 cm	150 cm
6.	Nadir measured the length of his paper. It is about . . .	2.85 mm	285 mm	28.5 mm
7.	The circumference of the playground ball is about . . .	5.8 dm	58 dm	580 dm
8.	Mikaela measured the width of her pencil box. It is about . . .	1.02 mm	10.2 mm	102 mm
9.	The distance from Omia's classroom to the gym is about . . .	4.0 m	40 m	400 m
10.	Blake measured the length of his foot. It was about . . .	14 dm	1.4 dm	0.14 dm

DO MORE

Choose one of the above problems. Explain how you chose the answer.

11

Name _____ Date _____

The Bugs Are Marching

Measure each line to the nearest centimeter. Measure each line to the nearest millimeter. Use the measurements to determine the length of each insect, using the Matrix Clues below and the chart on page 13.

1. ———————   _____ cm   _____ mm

2. ———————————   _____ cm   _____ mm

3. ———————————   _____ cm   _____ mm

4. ———   _____ cm   _____ mm

5. ———————————   _____ cm   _____ mm

6. ———————   _____ cm   _____ mm

Matrix Clues:

The number of millimeters in Red bug's length is divisible by 2.

When Purple bug's length is written using both centimeters and millimeters, it has a larger number in the centimeters place than in the millimeters place.

Green bug's length is less than 20 millimeters.

Red bug is not the smallest insect.

Orange bug's length is greater than 23 millimeters.

Blue bug is longer than orange bug.

Yellow bug's length is about half of blue bug's length.

0-7424-2895-8 *Using the Standards—Measurement*

Name _____ Date _____

The Bugs Are Marching (cont.)

Write the measure of each line from page 12 in the chart below. Write in centimeters to the nearest millimeter. For example, 44 mm is 4.4 cm.

	Line 1	Line 2	Line 3	Line 4	Line 5	Line 6
Blue bug						
Green bug						
Orange bug						
Purple bug						
Red bug						
Yellow bug						

1. Blue bug is _____

2. Green bug is _____

3. Orange bug is _____

4. Purple bug is _____

5. Red bug is _____

6. Yellow bug is _____

7. Draw a line the length of all six bugs combined. How long is it?

DO MORE

Double each bug's length. Write its new length and explain how you doubled.

0-7424-2895-8 *Using the Standards—Measurement*

Name _____ Date _____

Checking the Line

Use this line for the following measurements.

━━━━━━━━━━━━━━━

1. Measure to the nearest inch. _____

2. Measure to the nearest half inch. _____

3. Measure to the nearest quarter inch. _____

4. Measure to the nearest eighth inch. _____

5. Measure to the nearest sixteenth inch. _____

Use this line for the following measurements.

━━━━━━━━━━━━━━━━━

6. Measure to the nearest inch. _____

7. Measure to the nearest half inch. _____

8. Measure to the nearest quarter inch. _____

9. Measure to the nearest eighth inch. _____

10. Measure to the nearest sixteenth inch. _____

11. When would it be reasonable to measure to the nearest inch?

_____

_____

12. When would it be reasonable to measure to the nearest sixteenth inch?

_____

_____

DO MORE

Draw your own line. Measure to the nearest inch, half inch, quarter inch, eighth inch, and sixteenth inch. Explain the relationships among the measurements by using a chart. For example, one quarter inch equals two eighths.

14

Name _____ Date _____

From Volcanoes to the Ocean

Use the chart to answer the questions below. Show your work. Label your answers.

1 foot (ft.)	=	12 inches (in.)
1 yard (yd.)	=	3 feet (ft.)
1 mile (mi.)	=	1,760 yards (yd.)

1. Kilauea and Mauna Loa are volcanoes in Hawaii. Kilauea is about 4,090 feet above sea level. Mauna Loa is about 13,677 feet above sea level. Use the conversion chart above to find out if either volcano is more than a mile above sea level.

   Step one: Use the conversion chart above to determine the number of feet in a mile. Show your work.

   Step two: If a volcano has a height greater than 1 mile, write its height in miles, yards, and feet. If it is not greater than 1 mile, write its height in yards and feet. Show your work.

2. Dolphins, porpoises, and humpback whales are members of the whale family. A porpoise can be about 80 inches long. A dolphin can measure up to 360 inches. A humpback whale can measure up to 740 inches. Use the conversion chart to find out if any of these mammals are longer than a yard.

   Step one: Use the conversion chart above to determine the number of inches in a yard. Show your work.

   Step two: If one of these whales is greater than a yard, write its measure in yards, feet, and inches. If it is less than a yard, write its length in feet and inches. Show your work.

0-7424-2895-8 *Using the Standards—Measurement*

Name _____ Date _____

Crafters

Solve and show your work. Label your answers with the correct units.

1. On Monday Jade measured 356 inches of ribbon. On Tuesday she measured 127 inches, on Wednesday she measured 462 inches, and on Thursday she measured 198 inches of ribbon. How many inches of ribbon did she measure in all? Convert this answer to feet and inches.

2. Ian carved 25 feet of molding strip. He wants to cut this into 4-inch strips. How many 4-inch pieces can he cut?

3. Maegen can crochet 4 inches on her scarf in 1 hour. If she crochets $2\frac{1}{2}$ hours each day for 1 week, how long will her scarf be? Convert this answer to feet and inches.

When a scarf reaches 4 feet, Maegen starts a new one. How far has she gotten on the second scarf? How long will it take her to finish the second scarf?

DO MORE

Write an equation that shows the relationship between inches and feet.

Published by Instructional Fair. Copyright protected.

0-7424-2895-8 *Using the Standards—Measurement*

Metric Length Conversions

Fill in the blanks. Use the information to answer the questions below.

1 centimeter (cm)	=	10 millimeters (mm)
1 decimeter (dm)	=	10 centimeters (cm)
1 meter (m)	=	_____ millimeters (mm)
1 meter (m)	=	_____ centimeters (cm)
1 meter (m)	=	10 decimeters (dm)
1 decameter (dkm)	=	_____ centimeters
1 decameter (dkm)	=	_____ decimeters (dm)
1 decameter (dkm)	=	10 meters (m)
1 hectometer (hm)	=	100 meters (m)
1 hectometer (hm)	=	_____ decameters (dkm)
1 kilometer	=	1,000 meters (m)
1 kilometer	=	_____ decameters (dkm)
1 kilometer	=	_____ hectometers (hm)

1. Sydney's house is two houses away from the corner. She wants to measure the distance from her house to the corner. Which unit of measure should she use and why?

2. Dillon needs to measure the height of his dog. Which unit of measure should he use and why?

3. Anya is making a 5-meter paper chain. The chain is currently 34.3 decimeters long. How many more decimeters are needed? How many centimeters? How many meters?

4. Blake is biking to his grandmother's house. Her house is 7 kilometers away. He has already gone 210.7 decameters. How many more decameters must he pedal? How many meters? How many kilometers?

5. Madalen's plant is 7 centimeters tall. It grows 3 millimeters a day. How many millimeters tall will it be in one week? How many centimeters?

0-7424-2895-8 *Using the Standards—Measurement*

Name _____ Date _____

Around the Room, Metric Length

Look at the data collected in the table below. Fill in the missing columns. The first row is done for you.

1 meter	=	100 centimeters
1 decimeter	=	10 centimeters
1 centimeter	=	10 millimeters

Table One

Object	Millimeters	Centimeters	Decimeters	Meters
1. 6 dm	600	60	6	0.6
2. 23 mm				
3. 7.2 dm				
4. 54 cm				

Choose five objects of your own to fill in the chart below. Measure and fill in the table. Use your measurement to fill in each of the columns. Share your answers with a partner.

Table Two

Object	Millimeters	Centimeters	Decimeters	Meters
1.				
2.				
3.				
4.				
5.				

0-7424-2895-8 *Using the Standards—Measurement*

Name _____ Date _____

Longer and Shorter

You will need a variety of objects, a metric ruler, and a customary ruler.

1. Draw and label a line that is 4 inches long. Draw and label another that is 5 inches long.

Find 5 objects that are longer than 4 inches but less than 5 inches in length. List them here.

_____ _____ _____ _____ _____

Measure each to the nearest sixteenth of an inch. Record the measurement.

2. Draw and label a line that is 14 centimeters long. Draw and label another that is 15 centimeters long.

Find 5 objects that are longer than 14 centimeters, but less than 15 centimeters in length. List them here.

_____ _____ _____ _____ _____

Measure each to the nearest millimeter. Record the measurement.

DO MORE

Explain in writing how you found the objects for the activities above.

19

Name _____ Date _____

Can We Agree?

Measure these lines to the nearest millimeter. Compare your results with other students in the class. Find the range of results for each object. Record the range of the results on the lines below.

1. — measurement: _____ range: _____

2. - measurement: _____ range: _____

3. — measurement: _____ range: _____

4. — measurement: _____ range: _____

5. — measurement: _____ range: _____

6. — measurement: _____ range: _____

7. — measurement: _____ range: _____

8. — measurement: _____ range: _____

9. - measurement: _____ range: _____

10. — measurement: _____ range: _____

DO MORE

Explain what *range* means. Write an equation to show how you find it.

20

Name _____ Date _____

Accuracy Counts

You will need metric rulers and an object chosen by each student to measure.

Gather the students' objects. Choose which part of each object is to be measured. Label each object starting with number 1. Make a recording sheet for the measurements of these objects on a sheet of lined paper. Start with 1 on the first line and continue until each object has a place to record the measurement.

Start with your object. Measure to the nearest millimeter and record the measurement on the line with the object's number. Pass the objects until each student has had a chance to measure each object to the nearest millimeter and record the measurement. Be sure to record the measurement on the same line as the object's number. Find the range of results for each object.

O	1.	9 mm
	2.	
	3.	1.7 mm
O	4.	2 mm
	5.	
	6.	5.6 mm
O	7.	
	8.	3.8 mm

1. How do the ranges of measurements for the lines on page 20 compare to the range for the measurements of the objects on this page?

_____

_____

2. What are three things that may affect accuracy in measurement?

_____

_____

DO MORE

Repeat the activity with the same or different objects. This time, measure to the nearest $\frac{1}{16}$ of an inch.

0-7424-2895-8 *Using the Standards—Measurement*

Name _____ Date _____

Checking Angles

Measure the first four angles with a protractor. Write the angle degrees on the line.

1.
Straight Angle _____

3.  Circle _____

2.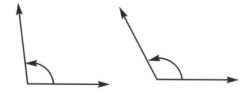
Right Angle _____

4. 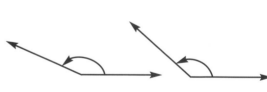 Reflex Angle _____

Acute Angles

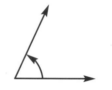 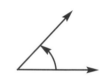

Reflex Angles

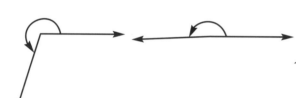  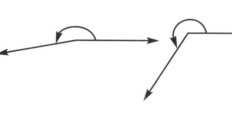

Obtuse Angles

Use the information above to help define each of the following types of angles.

acute angle: _____

_____

reflex angle: _____

_____

obtuse angle: _____

_____

0-7424-2895-8 *Using the Standards—Measurement*

Name _____ Date _____

Locating the Angles

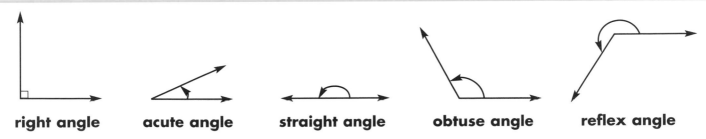

right angle   acute angle   straight angle   obtuse angle   reflex angle

Locate six of each of the following angles below. Trace each angle with the given color. Designate the space of the angle with a curved arrow.

acute angle: yellow
right angle: blue
obtuse angle: red
straight angle: purple
reflex angle: green

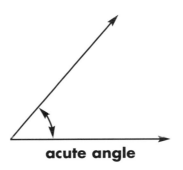

acute angle

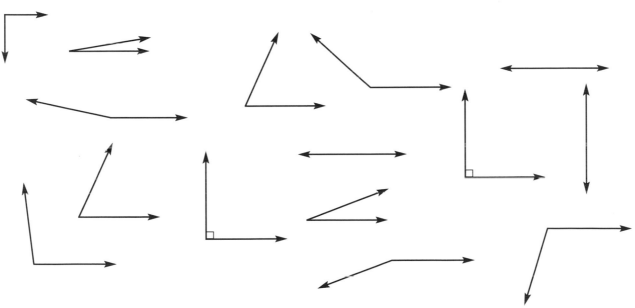

DO MORE

Make a tally chart to tally the number of angles found. Compare your angles with a partner. Who found the greatest number of each type of angle?

Name _____ Date _____

Measure the Angles

Measure each angle. Then identify each angle as *acute*, *right*, *obtuse*, *straight*, or *reflex*.

1. _____ _____

2. _____ _____

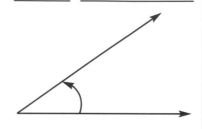

3. _____ _____

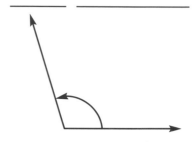

4. _____ _____

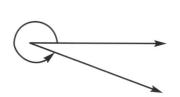

5. _____ _____

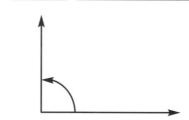

6. _____ _____

7. _____ _____

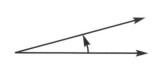

8. _____ _____

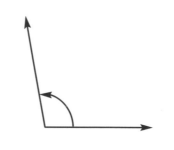

9. _____ _____

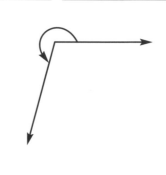

DO MORE

Write a definition for a reflex angle.

0-7424-2895-8 *Using the Standards—Measurement*

Name _____ Date _____

Scrutinizing Angles

Find the measure of each angle.

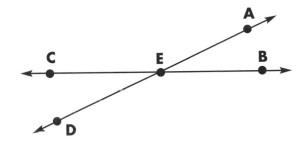

1. ∠AEB   _____

2. ∠BEC   _____

3. ∠AEC   _____

4. ∠CED   _____

5. ∠DEA   _____

6. ∠BED   _____

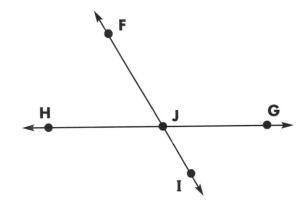

7. ∠FJG   _____

8. ∠GJH   _____

9. ∠FJH   _____

10. ∠HJI   _____

11. ∠IJF   _____

12. ∠GJI   _____

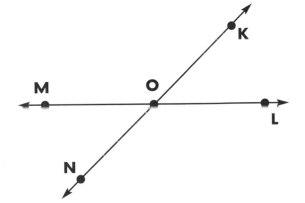

13. ∠KOL   _____

14. ∠LOM   _____

15. ∠KOM   _____

16. ∠MON   _____

17. ∠NOK   _____

18. ∠LON   _____

19. What patterns did you observe while measuring the above angles?

Can you write a rule to determine angle measurements of intersecting lines?

_____

_____

25

Angles in Shapes

Draw and label each shape with its given angle. Measure the remaining angles.

1. Draw triangle FUN. Angle ∠FUN is 60 degrees.

∠UNF _____   ∠NFU _____

2. Draw quadrilateral UNIT. Angle ∠NIT is 95 degrees.

∠ITU _____   ∠TUN _____   ∠UNI _____

3. Draw pentagon GREAT. Angle ∠EAT is 150 degrees.

∠ATG _____   ∠TGR _____

∠GRE _____   ∠REA _____

4. Draw hexagon ABCDEF. Angle ∠ABC is 200 degrees.

∠BCD _____   ∠CDE _____

∠DEF _____   ∠EFA _____

∠FAB _____

5. Draw octagon GHIJKLMN. Angle ∠GHI is 90 degrees.

∠HIJ _____   ∠IJK _____

∠JKL _____   ∠KLM _____

∠LMN _____   ∠MNG _____

∠NGH _____

0-7424-2895-8 *Using the Standards—Measurement*

Name _____ Date _____

Quadrilateral MATH

A. Look at quadrilateral MATH. Measure the angles and sides. Fill in the first row in the table below.

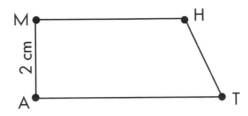

B. On another piece of paper draw other quadrilaterals labeled MATH. In each quadrilateral, angle MAT is 90 degrees and side MA is 2 centimeters. Record the measurements in the table.

∠MAT	∠ATH	∠THM	∠HMA	Side MA	Side AT	Side TH	Side HM
90°				2 cm			
90°				2 cm			
90°				2 cm			
90°				2 cm			
90°				2 cm			
90°				2 cm			
90°				2 cm			
90°				2 cm			
90°				2 cm			

1. Each quadrilateral MATH has one angle of 90 degrees and one side of 2 cm. Are the other angles in each figure equivalent? _____

2. Are the sides of each figure equivalent? _____

3. How are the quadrilaterals similar or different?

_____

_____

27

Name _____ Date _____

Within a Pentagon

Measure the angles of each pentagon. Record their measures within each angle. Find the sum of the angles in each pentagon and write it on the line. Hint: all pentagons have something in common.

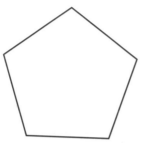

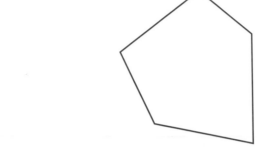

1. sum of angles _____

2. sum of angles _____

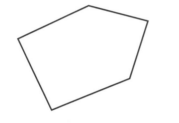

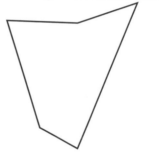

3. sum of angles _____

4. sum of angles _____

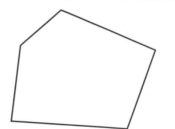

5. sum of angles _____

6. sum of angles _____

DO MORE

Explain how you know a pentagon. Draw one of your own.

Published by Instructional Fair. Copyright protected.

0-7424-2895-8 *Using the Standards—Measurement*

Name _____ Date _____

Within Shapes

Measure the angles of each shape. Record their measures within each angle. Find the sum of the angles, record their totals in the table. Make two irregular figures for each given shape. Label them figures B and C. Record the measures of their angles within the shapes. Record the sum of the angles in the table.

triangle A   quadrilateral A

hexagon A   octagon A

nonagon A   decagon A

shape	sum of angles figure A	sum of angles figure B	sum of angles figure C
1. triangle			
2. quadrilateral			
3. hexagon			
4. octagon			
5. nonagon			
6. decagon			

THINK

Collect additional data from classmates. What conclusions can you draw about the sums of different shapes' measures?

29

Name _____ Date _____

Who Made It?

Find the area and perimeter of each shape. Use the information and the clues to find out who made each shape. Create a problem-solving matrix if you need help solving.

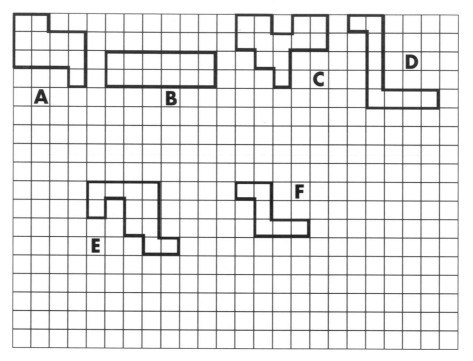

figure A: area _____   perimeter _____   made by _____

figure B: area _____   perimeter _____   made by _____

figure C: area _____   perimeter _____   made by _____

figure D: area _____   perimeter _____   made by _____

figure E: area _____   perimeter _____   made by _____

figure F: area _____   perimeter _____   made by _____

Eli, Zoë, and Abi each made a figure with the same perimeter.

Kay's figure has half the area of Val's figure.

Tam made a figure with the same area as Abi's figure.

The area of Zoë's figure is almost half its perimeter.

0-7424-2895-8 *Using the Standards—Measurement*

Name _____ Date _____

Museum Measurement

Solve each of the following problems. Use grid paper to help you. Design at least three figures that would fit the description. Sketch the figures to match the areas given. Label each perimeter. Attach the extra paper when handing in.

1. The metal edge-casing around the side of the mummy case needs to be replaced. The area of this section is 24 square feet. Determine the length of edging needed.

2. The cord used to keep visitors away from one of the large obelisks requires replacement. It borders an area that is 64 square feet. What length of cord is needed?

3. The museum is purchasing a security border for an area where visitors are not allowed. The area under security is 120 square feet. How much border is needed? What arrangement, using whole feet, would result in the smallest amount of border needed?

4. Curators need to build a wooden frame to border an area holding ancient artifacts. The artifacts fill a space that is 56 square feet. Determine the length of wooden frame needed.

THINK

Choose one of the problems above. How many different ways can you find to solve this problem? Show your solutions.

0-7424-2895-8 *Using the Standards—Measurement*

Name _____ Date _____

One Area

Draw at least six different figures using 10 adjoining squares. Write the area and perimeter next to each figure.

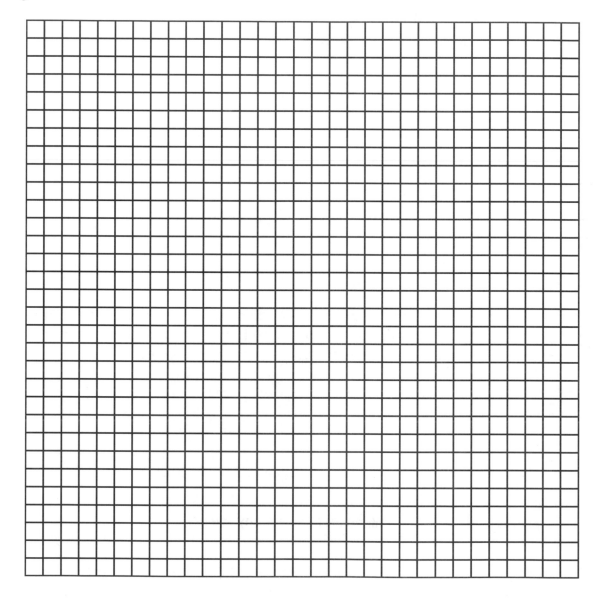

DO MORE

Explain what you discovered about the relationship between area and perimeter?

0-7424-2895-8 *Using the Standards—Measurement*

Name _____ Date _____

Grid Paper

Make the following figures on grid paper. Record your results next to the figure and on this page.

1. Create five different figures using 15 adjoining squares.

area _____   perimeter _____

area _____   perimeter _____

area _____   perimeter _____

area _____   perimeter _____

area _____   perimeter _____

2. Create five different figures using 24 adjoining squares.

area _____   perimeter _____

area _____   perimeter _____

area _____   perimeter _____

area _____   perimeter _____

area _____   perimeter _____

3. Create five different figures using 30 adjoining squares.

area _____   perimeter _____

area _____   perimeter _____

area _____   perimeter _____

area _____   perimeter _____

area _____   perimeter _____

4. Create five different figures using 36 adjoining squares.

area _____   perimeter _____

area _____   perimeter _____

area _____   perimeter _____

area _____   perimeter _____

area _____   perimeter _____

0-7424-2895-8 *Using the Standards—Measurement*

Name _____ Date _____

Around the Edge

Draw as many different figures as you can using the outside edge measurement given. Write the perimeter and area next to each figure. Record the perimeter, the largest and smallest areas, and the range of areas for each outside edge.

1. Outside edge of 4

perimeter _____

greatest area _____

smallest area _____

area range _____

2. Outside edge of 6

perimeter _____

greatest area _____

smallest area _____

area range _____

3. Outside edge of 8

perimeter _____

greatest area _____

smallest area _____

area range _____

4. Outside edge of 10

perimeter _____

greatest area _____

smallest area _____

area range _____

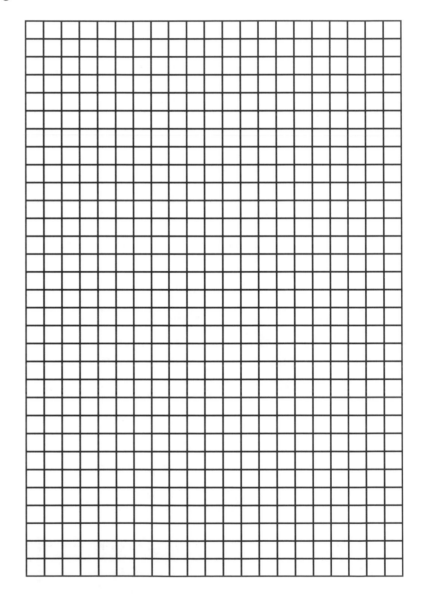

0-7424-2895-8 *Using the Standards—Measurement*

Name _____ Date _____

Perimeter

Make figures with the following perimeters on grid paper. Create figures with various areas for the same perimeter. Record areas and the range next to each figure. Share results with classmates.

Perimeter	Smallest Area	Greatest Area	Area Range
12			
14			
16			
18			
20			

DO MORE

 Have your thoughts about the relationship between perimeter and area changed? Record them.

0-7424-2895-8 *Using the Standards—Measurement*

Name _____ Date _____

Comparing Masses

Look at each pan balance. Which object has the most mass? Explain your answers.

1.

The object with the most mass is _____.

Explain your answer in writing or by creating a diagram.

_____

_____

2.

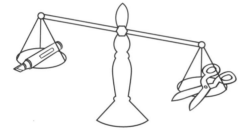

The object with the most mass is _____.

Explain your answer in writing or outloud.

_____

_____

3.

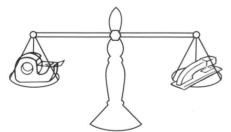

The object with the most mass is _____.

Explain your answer in writing.

_____

_____

36

Name _____ Date _____

Determining Masses

Look at the three pan balances. All the masses shown are in grams. Use the information to complete the directions given below.

Sketch a pan balance. Using what you learned from the illustrations above, put a cup on one pan and a washer on the other. Explain your drawing.

DO MORE

Choose three objects in your classroom. Compare their masses using a pan balance. Sketch them on balances. Order them from least to greatest mass. Explain your order.

37

Name _____ Date _____

Next Step

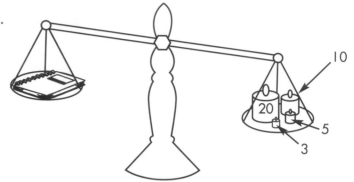

1. Jocelyn wants to balance the notebook.
What is the next step?

   a. add more mass

   b. take mass off pan

How much?

   a. 3 grams

   b. 5 grams

   c. 10 grams

   d. 20 grams

Explain your decision.

_____

_____

_____

_____

2. You have already tried adding another 20-gram mass.
Pan B ended up lower than Pan A.

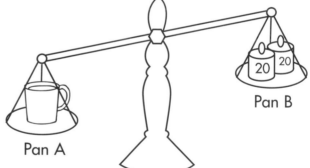

Pan B

Pan A

You want the cup to balance.
What is the next step?

   a. add more mass

   b. take mass off pan

How much?

   a. 1 gram

   b. 2 grams

   c. 10 grams

   d. 50 grams

Explain your decision.

_____

_____

_____

_____

0-7424-2895-8 *Using the Standards—Measurement*

Name _____ Date _____

Fresh Fruit

English System

1 pound (lb.) = 16 ounces (oz.)
1 ton (t.)   = 2,000 pounds (lb.)

Use the chart above to convert each measurement to ounces, then to pounds and ounces.

1. apples: $2\frac{1}{2}$ lb. 8 oz. _____ _____

2. blueberries: 2 lb. 20 oz _____ _____

3. bananas: $1\frac{1}{2}$ lb. 12 oz. _____ _____

4. peaches: $2\frac{3}{4}$ lb. 6 oz. _____ _____

5. plums: $1\frac{3}{4}$ lb. 13 oz. _____ _____

Use the clues to place the baskets of produce from above in order by drawing. The first basket of fruit is on the left.

The fruit with the most weight is not first or last. None of the baskets with a weight greater than 47 ounces are next to each other. The basket with the least weight is not second. The basket with 52 ounces of fruit in it is behind the basket with 41 ounces of fruit. The first basket has a weight that is equal to 3 pounds.

DO MORE

Use a Venn diagram to compare ounces, pounds, and tons.

0-7424-2895-8 *Using the Standards—Measurement*

Name _____ Date _____

Pounds and Kilograms

English System

I pound (lb.)	=	16 ounces (oz.)
I ton (t.)		= 2,000 pounds (lb.)

Metric System

I gram (g)	= 1,000 milligrams (mg)
I kilogram (kg)	= 1,000 grams (g)
I metric ton (t)	= 1,000 kilograms (kg)

Use the measurement tables above to complete the word problems. Show your work.

1. A full-grown gray wolf can weigh 1,508 ounces. How many pounds is this? _____

2. A worker bee collects enough nectar to make about 45 grams of honey in its lifetime. If a colony of bees can have about 24,286 worker bees, how many kilograms of honey could these bees make? _____

Convert to metric tons. _____

3. An ostrich egg is about 3 pounds How many ounces is this? _____

How many ounces is an egg that weighs $2\frac{3}{4}$ pounds? _____

How many ounces is a $3\frac{1}{8}$ -pound egg? _____

4. A whale shark can weigh about 39,897 pounds. Convert this to tons and pounds. _____

Average this to the nearest ton. _____

5. A male African elephant weighs about 5,426 kilograms. A male Indian elephant weighs about 3.6 metric tons. How much more is the African elephant? Give the answer in both metric tons and kilograms. _____ _____

0-7424-2895-8 *Using the Standards—Measurement*

Processes

Name _____ Date _____

Between the Grams

You will need a variety of objects and 2 pan balances and masses (or switch masses with one pan).

1. Place a 1-kilogram mass on one pan balance. Place a 2-kilogram mass on a second pan balance. Find 5 objects that are more than 1 kilogram and less than 2 kilograms. List them here.

_____ _____ _____ _____ _____

Now measure each to the nearest gram. Record your results. What is the range of measures? _____

2. Place a 10-gram mass on one pan balance. Place a 20-gram mass on a second pan balance. Find 5 objects that are more than 10 grams and less than 20 grams. List them here.

_____ _____ _____ _____ _____

Now measure each to the nearest gram. Record your results. What is the range of measures? _____

3. Place a 1-gram mass on one pan balance. Place a 2-gram mass on a second pan balance. Find 3 objects that are more than 1 gram, but less than 2 grams. List them here.

_____ _____ _____

What would you need to get a more exact measure of these objects? _____

_____

_____

DO MORE

Find three objects you believe are about the same mass. Measure each to the nearest gram. Discuss your results with a partner.

Name _____ Date _____

Exploring Volume

You need six different containers. They can be drinking glasses, jars, bowls, etc. Fill the containers with water, rice, cereal, and similar items.

Label the containers A, B, C, D, E, and F.

1. Which do you think holds the most or has the greatest volume? _____

Place the containers in order of predicted volume from greatest to least. Record your prediction here.

_____ _____ _____ _____ _____ _____

2. Make a plan for checking your prediction. You cannot use a graduated cylinder or a standard measuring device.

_____

_____

_____

_____

3. Carry out your plan. Place the containers in actual order from greatest to least volume. Record the results here.

_____ _____ _____ _____ _____ _____

DO MORE

Combine your 6 containers with those of a partner. Determine the order of volumes from greatest to least. Create a chart to record this data.

0-7424-2895-8 *Using the Standards—Measurement*

Name _____ Date _____

Varying Volume

Jacquelyn has six containers. She labeled them A through F. Use the clues below to show the water on the graduated cylinders at the correct level. Container D holds 60 mL.

A	B	C	D	E	F

Clues:

The volume of containers C and F equal the volume of container A.

Container C has half the volume of container D.

Container C is twice the volume of container F.

Container F has one-quarter the volume of container D.

Container E has the same volume as the total of containers B and C.

Container C is one-third the volume of container B.

Container E has double the volume of container D.

0-7424-2895-8 *Using the Standards—Measurement*

Name _____ Date _____

Finding the Volume of Objects

Find the volume of a variety of objects using a graduated cylinder. Determine the increments of each graduated cylinder. Use the increments to mark the requested amount. Use the pre-marked lines to answer the questions. Show your work.

1. The increments are _____ each.

Draw the original water line at 430 mL.
What is the water level at the pre-marked line?

_____

This is the water level after a marble is dropped in.
What is the volume of the marble? _____
Show your work.

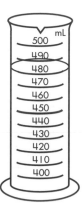

2. The increments are _____ each.

Draw the original water line at 72 mL.
What is the water level at the pre-marked line?

_____

This is the water level after a thumbtack
is dropped in. What is the volume of the
thumbtack? _____
Show your work.

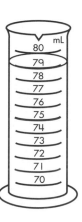

3. The increments are _____ each.

Draw the original water line at 165 mL.
What is the water level at the pre-marked line?

_____

This is the water level after a nail is dropped in.
What is the volume of the nail? _____
Show your work.

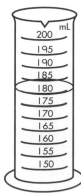

0-7424-2895-8 *Using the Standards—Measurement*

Name _____ Date _____

Capacity in the Grocery Aisle

Fill in the blanks in the measurement charts. Use the charts to answer the questions below. Show your work.

I tablespoon = 3 teaspoons
I cup = 16 tablespoons
I cup = _____ teaspoons
I cup = 8 fluid ounces
I pint = 2 cups
I pint = _____ fluid ounces
I quart = _____ cups

I quart = 2 pints
I quart = _____ fluid ounces
I gallon = _____ cups
I gallon = _____ pints
I gallon = 4 quarts
I gallon = _____ fluid ounces

1. Pia bought a I pint 8 ounce bottle of syrup. The label states that it is 2% real maple syrup. About how many ounces of real maple syrup are in the bottle? _____

2. Jade's family bought a canister of drink mix powder that will make 8 gallons. How many quarts is this? _____ How many ounces is it? _____

There are 5 people in Jade's family. Each person drinks two 16-ounce glasses a day. How much does the family drink in one day? _____ At this rate, how many days will one canister of drink mix last? _____

3. George is making a salad that calls for $1\frac{1}{2}$ cups of olive oil. The measuring cups are dirty, but not the measuring spoons. How many tablespoons of olive oil should he use for this recipe? _____ What if he used teaspoons instead? _____

George bought a 16-ounce bottle of olive oil. Will he have enough olive oil for the salad? Explain.

_____

_____

_____

_____

0-7424-2895-8 *Using the Standards—Measurement*

Name _____ Date _____

Metric Capacity

Use the chart to answer the questions below. Show your work.

1 teaspoon (tsp.) = 5 milliliters (mL)
1 tablespoon (Tbsp.) = 15 milliliters (mL)
1 liter (L) = 1,000 milliliters (mL)
1 liter (L) = 1,000 cubic centimeters (cm³)
1 liter (L) = 1 cubic decimeter (dm³)
1 liter (L) = 4 metric cups
1 kiloliter (kL) = 1,000 liters (L)

1. Marshall has a fish tank that holds 19 liters. He bought a rodent that needs 24,000 cubic centimeters of space. Is the tank large enough? Explain.

   _____

   _____

2. Kimber needs $2\frac{1}{5}$ tablespoons of cough syrup. How many milliliters should she take?

   _____

3. Ellis needs 1 metric cup of water for his recipe. How many tablespoons is this? _____ About how many teaspoons is it? _____

4. Leah bought a 3-liter bulk container of ketchup. She is using this to refill a 250 mL bottle. How many refills will she get out of the container? _____

5. Dillon's pool holds 6 kiloliters of water. Each month it needs 3 metric cups of chemicals for each 500 liters. How many liters of chemicals are needed? Explain how you arrived at your answer.

   _____

   _____

   _____

   _____

0-7424-2895-8 *Using the Standards—Measurement*

Name _____ Date _____

Looking at Thermometers

Look at each thermometer. Write the temperature in both Celsius and Fahrenheit.

1.

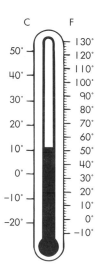

_____ _____

2.

_____ _____

3.

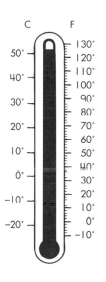

_____ _____

4.

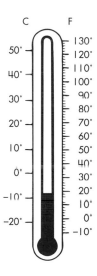

_____ _____

DO MORE

Look at each temperature. What would you plan to do if this was the outdoor temperature? Share your ideas with a partner. Make a list to hand in.

0-7424-2895-8 *Using the Standards—Measurement*

Name _____ Date _____

Planning Events

Look at each set of weather reports. Circle the day that would best fit the given situation. Use a thermometer with both the Celsius and Fahrenheit scales for reference.

1. Ian wants to go ice fishing. It is much easier to go when it is not snowing.

Monday	Tuesday	Wednesday	Thursday
–6°C Cloudy	5°C Cloudy	6°C Sunny	–5°C Sunny

Explain your choice. _____

_____

2. Maddie is planning a night to try out her new telescope and have a bonfire with her friends. She would like it cool, but not cold.

Thursday	Friday	Saturday	Sunday
3°C Clear	11°C Clear	21°C Clear	9°C Cloudy

Explain your choice. _____

_____

3. Maegen would like a hot day to go to the beach to swim. She does not want to get sunburned. Each of the following days report the weather and predicted water temperature in Lake Michigan.

Tuesday	Wednesday	Thursday	Friday
40°C Cloudy Water Temp 25°C	40°C Sunny Water Temp 15°C	20°C Cloudy Water Temp 25°C	30°C Sunny Water Temp 16°C

Explain your choice. _____

_____

0-7424-2895-8 *Using the Standards—Measurement*

Name _____ Date _____

Celsius and Fahrenheit

To change a Celsius temperature to Fahrenheit, use the following formula: $(1.8 \times °C) + 32 = °F$.

To change a Fahrenheit temperature to Celsius, use the following formula: $(°F - 32) \div 1.8 = °C$.

Use the formulas to change each temperature below to degrees on the alternate scale. Show your work. Check your answers with an actual thermometer.

1. $25°C =$ _____ $°F$

2. $55°C =$ _____ $°F$

3. $10°C =$ _____ $°F$

4. $-5°C =$ _____ $°F$

5. $68°F =$ _____ $°C$

6. $176°F =$ _____ $°C$

7. $95°F =$ _____ $°C$

8. $41°F =$ _____ $°C$

DO MORE

Write a paragraph that explains the relationship between degrees Fahrenheit and Celsius.

49

Name _____ Date _____

Wacky Weather

Find the temperature on each thermometer. Write the temperature using both the Fahrenheit and Celsius scales. Read the riddle. Figure out the new temperature and show it on the blank thermometer. Write the new temperature in both Fahrenheit and Celsius.

1.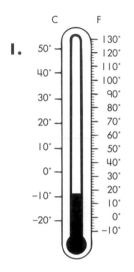

The temperature increased by 5 degrees Celsius, then by 10 degrees Celsius. The Celsius temperature then tripled. The temperature dropped 6 degrees Celsius then plummeted 25 degrees Celsius before warming up 6 degrees Celsius.

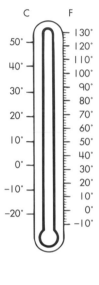

°C   °F

2.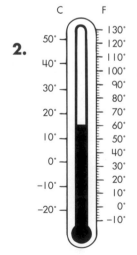

The temperature went up another 4 degrees Fahrenheit before dropping 10 degrees Fahrenheit. It dropped 2 degrees Fahrenheit each of the next 4 hours, then 5 degrees Fahrenheit the next 3 hours before going up 16 degrees. The temperature went up another 11 degrees Fahrenheit, then plummeted 43 degrees Fahrenheit.

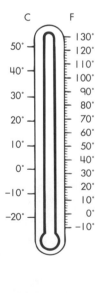

°C   °F

50

Name _____ Date _____

It's About Time

Use the information in the chart to answer the questions below. Show your work. Label your answers.

60 seconds = 1 minute	
60 minutes = 1 hour	
24 hours = 1 day	
7 days = 1 week	
52 weeks = 1 year	
365 days = 1 year	

1. A lemon shark grows a new set of teeth every 14 days. If this shark can grow up to 24,000 teeth in a year, about how many teeth are in each set? Explain how you arrived at your answer.

    _____

    _____

    _____

    _____

2. If you average 8 hours of sleep a night, how much time do you spend sleeping in 4 weeks? _____ About how many days is this? _____

3. A chimney swift (a type of bird) travels about 217,048 kilometers per year. At this rate, what would its weekly average be? _____

4. One species of bamboo can grow up to 2 feet in 12 hours. If it continued growing at this rate, how many feet tall would it be in 2 weeks? _____ How many yards? _____

51

Name _____ Date _____

As Time Goes By

Read each time given. Each time reads hours, then minutes, then seconds. Write the elapsed or predicted time and show it on the clock face.

1. It is 5:34:21. What time will it be in 1 hour, 3 minutes, and 45 seconds?   _____

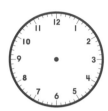

2. It is 10:55:47. What time will it be in 2 hours, 6 minutes, and 34 seconds?   _____

3. It is 8:17:39. What time will it be in 8 hours, 19 minutes, and 54 seconds?   _____

4. It is 6:42:57. What time will it be in 7 hours, 38 minutes, and 49 seconds?   _____

5. It is 4:28:06. What time was it 2 hours, 46 minutes, and 20 seconds ago?   _____

6. It is 11:13:31. What time was it 6 hours, 28 minutes, and 42 seconds ago?   _____

0-7424-2895-8 *Using the Standards—Measurement*

Name _____ Date _____

At the Zoo

Conver-Sion Zoo charted information about several of its animals. Convert the information in the chart. Convert height to yards. Convert weight to pounds.

Animal	Height/Length	Converted Height	Weight	Converted Weight
1. male ostrich	$7\frac{3}{4}$ feet	2 yd. 1 ft. 9 in.	5,520 ounces	345 lb.
2. male Indian elephant	$9\frac{1}{2}$ feet		4 tons	
3. male walrus	12 feet		$1\frac{1}{2}$ tons	
4. female walrus	8 feet		$1\frac{1}{4}$ tons	
5. hippopotamus	60 inches		$1\frac{3}{8}$ tons	
6. male giraffe	17 feet		1 ton 582 pounds	
7. male gorilla	75 inches		7,200 ounces	
8. male wolf	73 inches		1,296 ounces	
9. platypus	26 inches		83 ounces	
10. white rhinoceros	5 feet 7 inches		$3\frac{1}{2}$ tons	
11. Galapagos tortoise	48 inches		$\frac{3}{10}$ ton	
12. condor (wingspan)	$9\frac{1}{2}$ feet		368 ounces	

DO MORE

Continue this chart on another paper. Add information about six more animals that interest you. An encyclopedia is a good source of information.

0-7424-2895-8 *Using the Standards—Measurement*

Name _____ Date _____

At the Zoo (cont.)

Use the information in the table on page 53. Place the animal names in the Venn diagram below. Remember, placement can also be made in the outside set.

1.

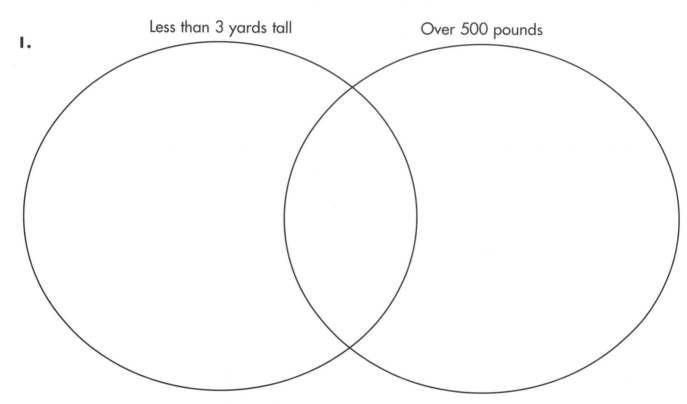

Less than 3 yards tall   Over 500 pounds

2. Choose one animal from each section of the Venn diagram. Explain its placement.

_____
_____
_____
_____
_____
_____
_____
_____
_____
_____

0-7424-2895-8 *Using the Standards—Measurement*

Name _____ Date _____

Finding the Same Amount

1. Draw a box around all amounts equal to 2 gallons 1 quart.

2. Draw a triangle around all amounts equal to 4 yards 2 feet.

3. Draw a ring around all amounts equal to 3 pounds 2 ounces.

4. Draw a star next to all amounts equal to $1\frac{1}{4}$ hours.

5. Underline all amounts equal to 1.327 decameters.

• 18 pints	• 8 quarts 4 cups
• 14 feet	• $4\frac{2}{3}$ yards
• 7 feet 84 inches	• $3\frac{1}{8}$ pounds
• 50 ounces	• 168 inches
• $2\frac{1}{2}$ pounds 10 ounces	• 75 minutes
• 69 minutes 360 seconds	• 1 hour 11 minutes 240 seconds
• 1,327 centimeters	• 0.1327 hectometers
• 132.7 decimeters	• 13.27 meters
• 1,327 millimeters	• 132.7 centimeters
• 1 gallon 4 pints	• $3\frac{1}{2}$ yards 36 inches
• 2 yards 24 feet 12 inches	• 5 quarts 6 pints
• 48 ounces	• $1\frac{1}{4}$ pounds 25 ounces
• 73 minutes 60 seconds	• $\frac{3}{4}$ hour 20 minutes
• 34 cups 1 pint	• 168 inches

0-7424-2895-8 *Using the Standards—Measurement*

Name _____ Date _____

Ridiculous or Reasonable

Read each situation. Determine which answer is ridiculous and which is reasonable. Place an X on the ridiculous answer.

1.	length of a pencil allowed in a pencil sharpener	millimeters	meters
2.	weight of an elephant	ounces	tons
3.	time it takes to blink	seconds	hours
4.	height of a volcano	inches	yards
5.	volume of an individual juice box	teaspoons	pints
6.	mass of a vitamin	milligrams	kilograms
7.	distance a bus travels in one hour	meters	kilometers
8.	length of a school year	minutes	months
9.	mass of a small paper clip	grams	kilograms
10.	length of a river	yards	miles
11.	capacity of a gas tank	microliters	liters
12.	weight of a newborn baby	kilograms	grams
13.	mass of an ice cream cone	ounces	pounds
14.	length between tires on a bike	inches	yards

DO MORE

List one object that could be measured with each of the following units: tons, miles, milliliters, days, decimeters, kilograms, and quarts. Do not write any that are ridiculous.

56

Name _____ Date _____

Public Measurement

You will need a variety of foods or safe unopened cleaning products and measuring tools.

Choose five products. Look at each product label. Identify what is being measured, for example, length, capacity, or weight. Determine the appropriate tools needed to check for accuracy. Record the information in the table below using appropriate units.

Product Name	Type of Measurement	Measurement Tool	Stated Measurement	Student Measurement

1. How close are your measurements to the measurements stated on the products?

_____

_____

2. What does this tell you about precision in measurement?

_____

_____

_____

DO MORE

Choose one of the above products. Re-measure the product using a more precise measurement. For example, instead of liters use milliliters. Explain why this is more accurate.

57

Name _____   Date _____

Create Your Own Problems I

1. Choose a type and unit of measurement and measure several objects. Write a statement about your measurement on an index card. Provide three measurement choices across the bottom of the card. One choice is correct, the other two are incorrect. Put a paper punch below each answer choice. On the back, make a circle around the correct choice. For self-correction, the student will place a pointed object (such as a sharpened pencil) through the paper punch hole, flip the card, and see which answer is correct. Swap your cards with other students.

2. Using a variety of linear metric measures, measure ten objects. Use the measurements to create a table with the following headings: Object, Measurement, and Unit. Leave the unit column blank for another student to fill in. Make an answer key to go with your table.

3. Create self-checking angle cards. Make 15 angle cards for each type of angle: acute, right, obtuse, straight, and reflex. Write the angle measurement on one side and the angle type on the other. Trade with a partner for angle practice or combine sets to make a large pack of angle cards.

4. Make a list of measures used in your daily life. Include examples from the following areas: length, temperature, angles, mass, weight, time, perimeter, and capacity.

5. Make a measurement poster. Include types of measurements, tools for measuring, and units of measure. Design an assessment attribute check list for this poster in a small group or as a class. This list should include the quality of the project as well as the number of required items needed.

58

Create Your Own Problems II

1. List a variety of real-life measurements: lengths, weights, temperatures, etc. Write at least two equivalent conversions for each.

2. Use a calendar to determine your current age to the nearest day. Convert this to weeks. Then convert to days, hours, minutes, and finally, to seconds.

3. Choose an area. Using that area, make as many different figures on grid paper as you can. Find the perimeter of each figure. Compare with a partner who used the same area and then compile your results. Repeat for a variety of areas. How does the size of the area affect the number of different figures you can make?

4. Prove that figures with the same area may not have the same perimeter. Develop an experiment and carry it out.

5. What happens to the sum of the angles as you change the size of a shape, but not the number of sides? Provide proof for your solution.

6. Begin with an area of 1 square unit. Draw as many different figures on grid paper as you can with this area. Continue with each number, 1 through 9. Make a table or other recording device to show your results. What patterns and relationships have you found?

0-7424-2895-8 *Using the Standards—Measurement*

Name _____ Date _____

Check Your Skills

Measure these two lines to the nearest $\frac{1}{16}$ inch.

1. ━━━━━━━━━━━━━━━━━━━━━ _____

2. ━━━━━━━━━━━━━━━━━ _____

Measure these two lines to the nearest millimeter.

3. ━━━━━━━━━━━ _____

4. ━━━━━━━━━━━━━━━ _____

5. What are the increments of this
graduated cylinder? _____

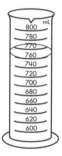

Draw the original water line at 680 mL.
What is the water level at the pre-marked line? _____

This is the water level after a marble is dropped in.

What is the volume of the marble? _____
Show your work.

6. Write the temperature shown in Celsius and Fahrenheit. _____ _____

Draw an example of each of the following angles.

7. acute

8. obtuse

9. reflex

10. right

11. straight

12. What information does the pan balance
give you about the banana and the grapes?

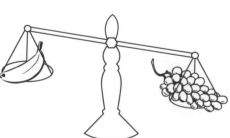

_____

_____

_____

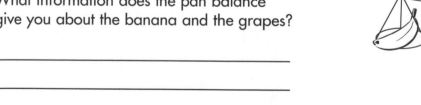

60

Check Your Skills (cont.)

13. The width of a pencil is 7 mm. This is equal to: _____ cm _____ dm _____ m

14. The height of a window is 3.5 meters. This is equal to: _____ mm _____ cm _____ dm

15. The length of a driveway is 40 yards. This is equal to: _____ inches _____ feet

16. The bucket has 88 ounces of blueberries in it. This is equal to: _____ pounds

17. The boulder weighed 4,500 kilograms. This is equal to: _____ grams _____ metric tons

18. Two gallons of water are in the bowl. This is equal to:

_____ fluid ounces _____ cups _____ pints _____ quarts

19. The bucket has 50 liters of water in it. This is equal to: _____ milliliters _____ kiloliters

20. It took 5 weeks to finish the project. This is equal to: _____ hours _____ days

21. Answer the following without using a protractor. Angle ∠AEB is 100 degrees.

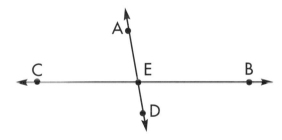

What is the measure of angle ∠BEC? _____

angle ∠AEC? _____

angle ∠CED? _____

angle ∠DEA? _____

angle ∠BED? _____

0-7424-2895-8 *Using the Standards—Measurement*

Name _____ Date _____

Grab a Meter Stick

The class recorded the following measurements. The students forgot to add the units when measuring. All students used a metric measuring tool. Determine whether **millimeters**, **centimeters**, **decimeters**, or **meters** were used. Then convert all measurements to centimeters. Write that measurement in the Conversion column of the table.

1 mm
-
1 cm
_____
1 dm

Object	Measurement	Unit	Conversion
1. new pencil length	1.8		
2. desk top width	520		
3. student height	15.1		
4. door height	2.03		
5. calculator length	126		
6. soda can circumference	2.5		

DO MORE

Choose one problem from above. Explain your unit choice.

0-7424-2895-8 *Using the Standards—Measurement*

Name _____ Date _____

Looking at Length

1. Without using a ruler, draw a line you believe is 1 centimeter long.

2. Now draw a line you believe is 1 inch long.

3. Measure each line with a ruler. To the nearest millimeter, how long is the first line you drew? _____

How close, in millimeters, is your estimate to an actual centimeter? _____

4. To the nearest $\frac{1}{16}$ of an inch, how long is your second line? _____

How close, to the nearest $\frac{1}{16}$ inch, is your estimate to an actual inch? _____

Estimate the measures of six objects. Record your estimates in the table. Then measure each object first to the nearest millimeter, then to the nearest $\frac{1}{16}$ inch. Add this information to the table.

Object	Centimeter Estimate	Actual Measure	Inch Estimate	Actual Measure
my pencil				
my desk				

63

0-7424-2895-8 *Using the Standards—Measurement*

Name _____ Date _____

Angle Work

Identify each angle as *acute*, *right*, *obtuse*, *straight*, or *reflex*. Estimate the measure of each. Then find the actual measure.

1.

angle type _____ estimated measure _____ actual measure _____

2.

angle type _____ estimated measure _____ actual measure _____

3.

angle type _____ estimated measure _____ actual measure _____

4.

angle type _____ estimated measure _____ actual measure _____

5.

angle type _____ estimated measure _____ actual measure _____

6.

angle type _____ estimated measure _____ actual measure _____

7.

angle type _____ estimated measure _____ actual measure _____

8.

angle type _____ estimated measure _____ actual measure _____

0-7424-2895-8 *Using the Standards—Measurement*

Name _____ Date _____

The Proper Angle

Use this page with page 66. Measure the following angles. Remember, a straight line equals 180 degrees.

1. ∠CLA _____
2. ∠TLA _____
3. ∠MLA _____
4. ∠ZLA _____
5. ∠YLA _____

6. Is angle ∠ZLA right, acute, obtuse or reflex? Prove it without measuring angle ∠ZLA.

_____

7. Is angle ∠ALY 30 degrees or 190 degrees? Explain without measuring angle ∠ALY.

_____
_____
_____
_____

8. Add an angle ∠JLA that is 70 degrees. Use a protractor.

9. Find the measure of angle ∠ZLY without measuring angle ∠ZLY. Explain.

_____
_____
_____
_____

10. Find the measure of angle ∠ALM without measuring angle ∠ALM. Explain.

_____
_____
_____
_____
_____
_____
_____
_____

0-7424-2895-8 *Using the Standards—Measurement*

Name _____ Date _____

The Proper Angle (cont.)

Use the figure below to answer the questions on page 65.

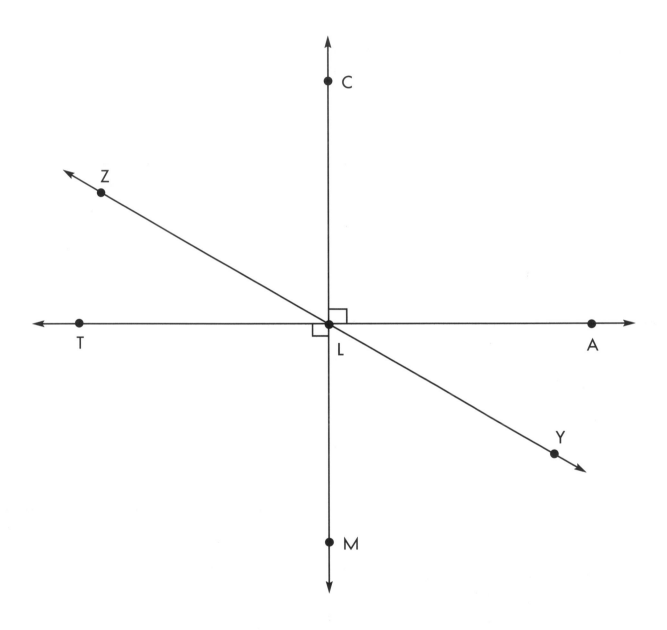

0-7424-2895-8 *Using the Standards—Measurement*

Name _____ Date _____

Estimating Perimeter

Cut four 1-centimeter wide strips of paper. Using centimeter grid paper will make this easy. These will be used during the activity below.

Estimate the perimeter of each figure on the grid. Use the centimeter grid strips as guides. Write the estimate next to the figure. Place the centimeter strip on its edge around the perimeter of the figure (like a fence). Is it longer or shorter than the figure?

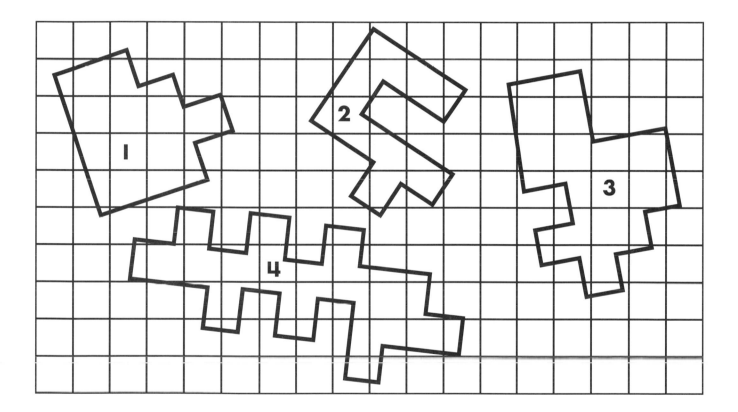

Figure 1: estimated perimeter _____   longer   shorter

Figure 2: estimated perimeter _____   longer   shorter

Figure 3: estimated perimeter _____   longer   shorter

Figure 4: estimated perimeter _____   longer   shorter

0-7424-2895-8 *Using the Standards—Measurement*

Comparing Perimeter Estimates

Draw four irregular shapes on a piece of centimeter grid paper. Label the figures A–D. Find the estimated perimeter and area of each. Record the estimates below in the table. Then find the actual perimeters and areas and record. Finally, find the average and range of the actual measures.

	Figure A	**Figure B**	**Figure C**	**Figure D**
Est. Perimeter				
Est. Area				
Act. Perimeter				
Act. Area				

Perimeter

Average _____   Range _____

Area

Average _____   Range _____

DO MORE

Use a centimeter strip the length of the average to compare to the shapes. Is it longer or shorter?

0-7424-2895-8 *Using the Standards—Measurement*

Name _____ Date _____

Round and Round

The distance around a figure is the perimeter. Estimate the distance around the figures below, then calculate the actual perimeter. Don't forget to label the units.

1.

28 cm | 46 cm (rectangle)

estimate _____   actual _____

2.

13 in. hexagon (all sides 13 in.)

estimate _____   actual _____

3.

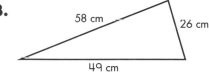

58 cm, 26 cm, 49 cm triangle

estimate _____   actual _____

4.

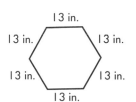

106 m, 45 m, 67 m, 85 m, 72 m

estimate _____   actual _____

5.

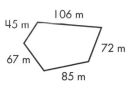

14 yd., 7 yd., 7 yd., 4 yd., 4 yd., 7 yd., 7 yd., 14 yd.

estimate _____   actual _____

6.

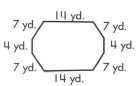

249 mm square

estimate _____   actual _____

0-7424-2895-8 *Using the Standards—Measurement*

Name _____ Date _____

The Area of a Thing

1. Ian cut a 5 by 3 section from grid paper and labeled it figure A.

What is the area of this figure? _____

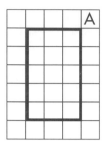

2. Next he tore part of the top left side off and called the new figure (figure B).

Ian knows that the new figure cannot have an area greater than figure A. He looked at the part he tore off. How many full squares were cut off? _____

Subtract this from the area of figure A. _____ The area of figure B cannot be larger than this difference.

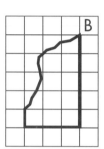

3. Next, Ian traced a line around all of the whole squares in figure B and called this portion figure C.

The area of figure C is _____. The area of figure B cannot be less than this.

Review: the area of figure B must be between _____ and _____.

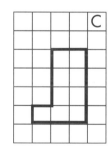

4. Finally he looked for parts that could make about a full square when put together. He found three parts he thought would be about one square and labeled them both I. He found two parts he thought would make about one square and labeled them II.

How many additional squares did he make? _____

Ian added the additional squares to the area of figure C to find his estimated area of figure B. Show the work he did.

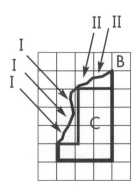

0-7424-2895-8 *Using the Standards—Measurement*

Techniques and Tools

Name _____ Date _____

Step on It

Trace your shoe on a piece of grid paper. Find the estimated area. Record below in the first table, first box. Form a group of 4 or 5 students. Look at the estimated area of each shoe. Record each person's measure in a block of the first table and label with the student's name. Find the average area of the shoes. Record it in the table. Write the range under the table. Repeat for each table.

Foot with Shoe   Average

Range: _____

Foot with Sock   Average

Range: _____

Hand   Average

Range: _____

DO MORE

Compare your results with other groups. Discuss your thoughts about estimating the area of irregular shapes.

0-7424-2895-8 *Using the Standards—Measurement*

Name _____ Date _____

More Things to Step On

1. Trace your shoe on a piece of construction paper or card stock.

2. Trace your shoe shape onto pieces of small, medium, and large square grid paper.

3. Find the area of the shoe on the grid paper with the large squares. _____

4. Find the area of the shoe on the grid paper with the medium squares. _____

5. Find the area of the shoe on the grid paper with the small squares. _____

6. Trade with at least one other person. Find the different areas of that person's shoe. Place that information in the table below.

7. Find the average and range of measures for each size of grid paper square. Record in the table.

8. Share more information to complete the table.

	Large Squares	Medium Squares	Small Squares
my shoe			
_____'s shoe			
_____'s shoe			
_____'s shoe			
_____'s shoe			
_____'s shoe			
_____'s shoe			
_____'s shoe			
_____'s shoe			
_____'s shoe			
average			
range			

THINK

What conclusions can you make about estimating area and the size of the units used to measure? Write your thoughts and share with classmates.

Published by Instructional Fair. Copyright protected.

0-7424-2895-8 *Using the Standards—Measurement*

Name _____ Date _____

More Things to Measure

Find the estimated area of each of the following shapes. State the estimated range of the area. ("between _____ and _____") Write a number sentence showing *whole units + parts = area* on the second line.

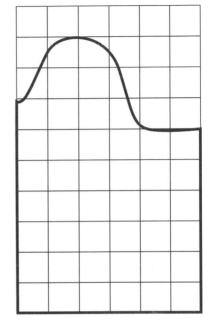

Figure 1

between _____ and _____

_____

Figure 2

between _____ and _____

_____

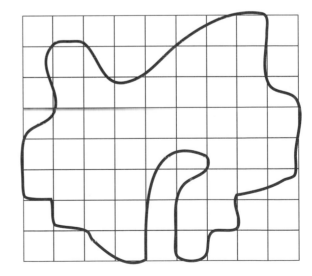

DO MORE

Compare your estimated areas with a partner. Did you both combine the same parts to make wholes? How did differences affect your totals?

0-7424-2895-8 *Using the Standards—Measurement*

Name _____ Date _____

Looking at the Whole

1. Build a figure out of centimeter cubes that is 4 x 4 x 4. What is the area of this figure? Remember to label with cubic centimeters. _____

2. Build a second figure that is 5 x 5 x 5 cubic centimeters. What is the area of this figure? _____

3. Find seven objects that you believe have a volume in between the volumes of the two figures you created above. Place them in order from least to greatest volume. Sketch and label the figures.

4. Use the centimeter cubes from the 5 x 5 x 5 figure to build a figure similar in size and shape to each of your sketched figures. Write your estimated volume below each sketch. Make any adjustments in order by numbering them 1 through 7 with 1 being smallest volume and 7 being greatest. Trade with a partner. Estimate the volume of these shapes. Compare the estimated volumes of the 14 shapes.

DO MORE

Write a conclusion about estimating volume with cubic centimeter cubes.

0-7424-2895-8 *Using the Standards—Measurement*

Name _____ Date _____

Area Exponent

An exponent is a number that tells how many times the base is used as a factor. An exponent can be used to find the area of a square.

$4 \times 4 = 4^2 = 16$ square units

Look at each figure. Write a multiplication problem to find the area.

1.

7 ft.

_____

2.

4 m

_____

3.

9 in.

_____

4.

5 yd.

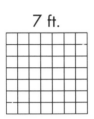

_____

5.   11 mm

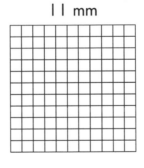

_____

6.   15 dm

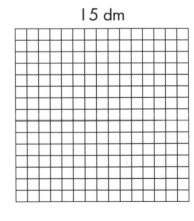

_____

Find the perimeter of each figure above.

1. _____   **2.** _____   **3.** _____   **4.** _____   **5.** _____   **6.** _____

0-7424-2895-8 *Using the Standards—Measurement*

Name _____ Date _____

Exploring Rectangular Area

Use the dimensions to find the area of each figure. Write the area on the line.

1. length _____ height _____ area _____

2. length _____ height _____ area _____

3. length _____ height _____ area _____

4. length _____ height _____ area _____

5. length _____ height _____ area _____

6. length _____ height _____ area _____

7. length _____ height _____ area _____

8. length _____ height _____ area _____

DO MORE

What is the relationship between the length, height, and area? Write a number sentence showing this relationship.

0-7424-2895-8 *Using the Standards—Measurement*

Name _____ Date _____

More Rectangles

Use the formula *length x height* = *area* to find the area of each figure. Show your work. Write your answers in square units.

1. _____

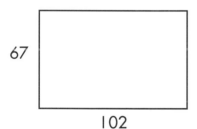

32

79

2. _____

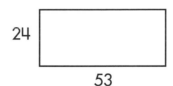

24

53

3. _____

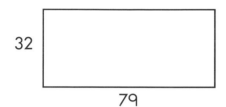

67

102

4. _____

49

237

5. _____

91

148

6. _____

85

452

DO MORE

Double the length, but not the height. Explain what happens to the area of each figure.

0-7424-2895-8 *Using the Standards—Measurement*

Name _____ Date _____

Exploring the Area of Parallelograms

Use the parallelogram and the grid squares to help you answer the questions.

1. Meg looked at the parallelogram above to find a way to find its area. First she looked at the base, or bottom, of the parallelogram. How long is it? _____

2. Next she looked at how high the parallelogram is. How high is it? _____

3. Next she found the largest rectangular part that she could. She labeled it A. What is the area of A? _____

4. She labeled the triangle to the left of the rectangle B. What is the area of this triangle? _____

5. She then labeled the remaining triangle C and found its area. It is _____.

6. She noticed a relationship between triangle B and triangle C. What is the relationship?

    _____

7. Take the area made by triangle B and draw it next to triangle C. What shape does it make?

    _____

8. The area of a rectangle is *length x height*. How does this relate to the formula for a parallelogram, which is *base x height*?

    _____

    _____

    _____

    _____

    _____

0-7424-2895-8 *Using the Standards—Measurement*

Name _____ Date _____

Rectangles and Parallelograms

Determine the area of each figure. Show your work.

Area of rectangle: *length x height*

Area of parallelogram: *base x height*

I. _____

28

39

2. _____

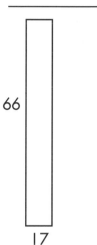

66

17

3. _____

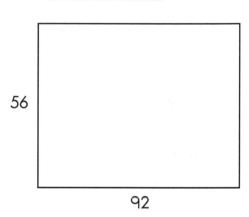

56

92

4. _____

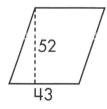

52

43

5. _____

26

81

6. _____

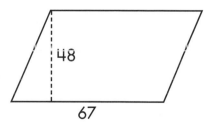

48

67

DO MORE

Double both the length and the height or the base and the height. Explain what happens to the area of each figure.

79

Name _____ Date _____

Shadows Within Shadows

Determine the area of each figure. Show your work.

Area of triangle: $\frac{1}{2}$ *base x height*

Area of rectangle: *length x height*

Area of parallelogram: *base x height*

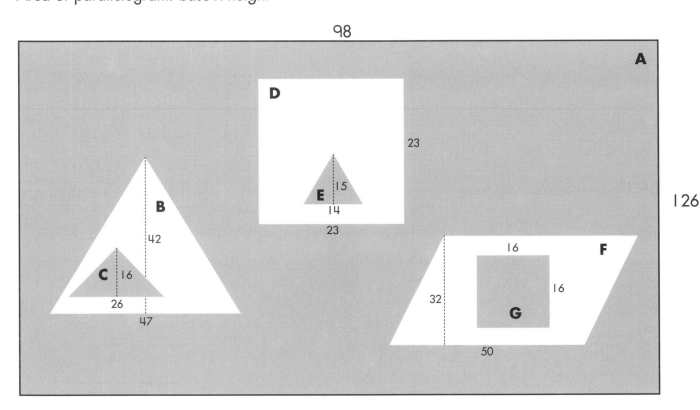

1. Find the total area of rectangle A. _____

2. Find the area of each individual figure. B _____ C _____ D _____

   E _____ F _____ G _____

3. What is the area of A without the white internal triangle? _____

4. What is the area of only the white parts of the whole figure? _____

5. What is the area of all the shaded sub-parts of the figure? _____

0-7424-2895-8 *Using the Standards—Measurement*

Name _____ Date _____

Irregular Towers

Build each figure with cubes. Find volume and surface area. Remember, each exposed side of a cube must be counted to find the surface area.

Figure A

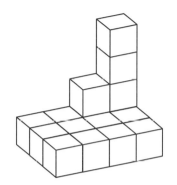

volume _____

surface area _____

Figure B

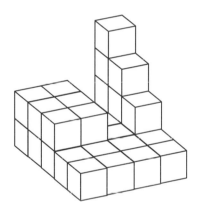

volume _____

surface area _____

Figure C

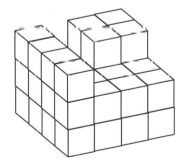

volume _____

surface area _____

DO MORE

Use 20 blocks. Build an irregular figure. Find its surface area. How many different surface areas can you find for this volume? Record your results in a chart.

0-7424-2895-8 *Using the Standards—Measurement*

Name _____ Date _____

Building Towers

Volume is the number of cubes used to make the object.
Surface area is the sum of the areas of each face.

Use cubes to build the following towers. Continue building towers, adding one level each time.
Fill in the table.

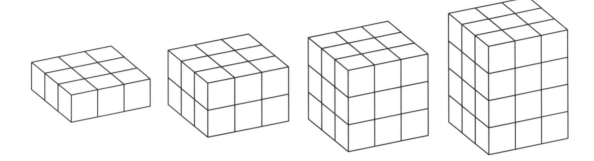

Height of Tower (units)	1	2	3	4	5	6	7	8
Volume of Tower (cubic units)								
Surface Area of Tower (square units)								

Describe any patterns you notice.

_____

_____

_____

_____

_____

_____

82

Name _____ Date _____

Covering Cubes

1. Follow the directions to find the surface area of a cube-shaped box that has a side length of 3 centimeters.

   a. Use centimeter cubes to make a solid figure that is 3 centimeters long, 3 centimeters wide, and 3 centimeters high. How many cubes did you use? _____

   b. Draw a square on a piece of paper that will exactly cover the top. How long is each side of the square? _____ What is the area of this side? _____

   c. Draw a square that will cover each of the other sides. What is the length of each side? _____ What is the width of each square? _____ How many of these squares do you need? _____

   d. Find the area of each square you drew to cover the sides. Write the area in the middle of each square.

   e. Write an addition sentence that will find the total surface area of this cube.

   _____

   _____

   f. Write a multiplication sentence to find the total surface area of this cube.

   _____

   _____

2. If a side = s, and the surface area = SA, what equation could you write to find the surface area of a cube? _____

DO MORE

Build a variety of cubes with centimeter blocks. Find the surface area of these cubes. Compare your results with a partner. Check for accuracy.

0-7424-2895-8 *Using the Standards—Measurement*

Name _____ Date _____

Covering Boxes

Build each figure. Find the area of each side. Add the areas of the six sides to find the surface area of each rectangular prism.

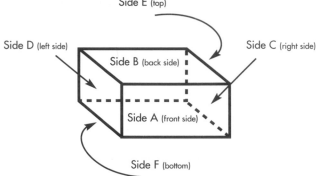

Figure A

length = 6   width = 5   height = 3

area of side A _____
area of side B _____
area of side C _____
area of side D _____
area of side E _____
area of side F _____
Total surface area _____

Figure B

length = 3   width = 7   height = 4

area of side A _____
area of side B _____
area of side C _____
area of side D _____
area of side E _____
area of side F _____
Total surface area _____

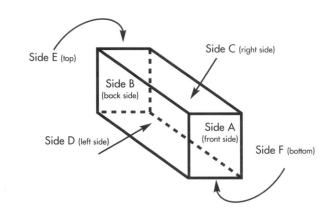

Figure C

length = 8   width = 2   height = 4

area of side A _____
area of side B _____
area of side C _____
area of side D _____
area of side E _____
area of side F _____
Total surface area _____

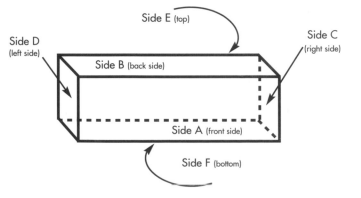

Using the information you gathered, what formula can you use to find the total surface area of a box?

_____

_____

Published by Instructional Fair. Copyright protected.   0-7424-2895-8 *Using the Standards—Measurement*

Name _____ Date _____

Filling Cubes

1. Follow the directions to find the volume of a cube-shaped box that has a side length of 4 centimeters.

    a.   Draw a 4 cm square on a piece of paper. Trace and cut to make six 4 by 4 cm square pieces of paper.

    b.   Set one square on your desk. This is the bottom of the box. Cover with one-centimeter cubes.

        How many one-centimeter cubes cover the bottom of the box? _____

    c.   Hold another square at a 90 degree angle along a side of the base. Continue stacking layers of one-centimeter cubes until they reach the height of this side.

        How many times did you repeat the first layer to fill this box? _____

    d.   Lay one of your paper squares on top of the cubes. Hold the other 4 by 4 cm sides to complete the box. You have now constructed a model of a box.

        What is the total number of cubes that fit in the box? _____
        Show your work.

        What measurement did you just find? _____

2. If a side = s and the total number of cubes = c, what equation could you write to find the volume of a cube? _____

3. Find the area of each square used. _____

    Add the totals to find the surface area of this figure. _____

DO MORE

    How many cubes would fit inside other cube-shaped boxes? Compare your results with a partner. Check for accuracy.

       0-7424-2895-8 *Using the Standards—Measurement*

Name _____ Date _____

Filling More Boxes

Follow the directions to find the volume of a rectangular prism.

Figure A

1. Make a base that is 3 cubes long and 2 cubes wide. How many cubes did you use? _____

2. Add another layer of cubes. How many cubes high is this rectangular prism? _____
   How many cubes in this layer? _____ What is the total number of cubes? _____

Figure B

3. Make a base that is 4 cubes long and 3 cubes wide. How many cubes did you use? _____

4. Add another layer of cubes. How many cubes are in this layer? _____

   What is the total number of cubes? _____

5. Add another layer of cubes. How many cubes high is this rectangular prism? _____
   How many cubes are in this layer? _____ What is the total number of cubes? _____

Record the measurements for figures A and B. Make the remaining figures and record
their volume.

Figure A: length = _____ width = _____ height = _____ volume = _____

Figure B: length = _____ width = _____ height = _____ volume = _____

Figure C: length = 3 cm width = 5 cm height = 2 cm volume = _____

Figure D: length = 2 cm width = 4 cm height = 6 cm volume = _____

6. Using the information you gathered, what formula could you construct to find the volume of
   a box? Explain the formula *l x w x h = v*.

   _____

   _____

   _____

7. Explain why the label for volume is *cubic units*.

   _____

   _____

   _____

0-7424-2895-8 *Using the Standards—Measurement*

Name _____ Date _____

Centimeter Cube Figures

Construct the following figures using 1-centimeter cubes. Complete the empty spaces in the table. Write the volume in cubic centimeters. Construct your own figures to fill in the final portions of the table.

	Length	Width	Height	Volume	Surface Area
1.	2	2	2		
2.	3	2	5		
3.	4	5	2		
4.	8		2	48 cm³	
5.		3	7	63 cm³	
6.	2	2		28 cm³	
7.				24 cm³	
8.					88 cm²

9. Using the information you gathered, look for a relationship between volume and surface area. Explain what you found.

_____

_____

_____

_____

_____

_____

DO MORE

Make your own figures. Using the information gathered from your own figures, leave out one number and have a partner find the missing data.

87

Name _____ Date _____

Riddles

Read each of the following riddles. Make a sketch showing a figure that would fit the given criteria. Label the drawing.

1. I am a figure with a volume of 24 cubic units. What is my length _____, width _____, height _____, and surface area _____?

2. I am a figure with a volume of 120 cubic units. What is my length _____, width _____, height _____, and surface area _____?

3. I am a figure with a volume of 64 cubic units. What is my length _____, width _____, height _____, and surface area _____?

4. I am a figure with a volume of 86 cubic units. What is my length _____, width _____, height _____, and surface area _____?

DO MORE

Make a table to collect data for the above figures. Collect information from your classmates and compare.

Name _____ Date _____

Volume and Surface Area Exponents Table

Fill in the table. Use exponents to write the formulas. Build the first 5 figures, then record your results. Build the remaining figures or use the formulas to fill in the rest of the chart. The first row has been done for you.

Cubic Figure	Representation for Volume	Volume	Representation for the Area of One Side	Area of One Side	Formula for Surface Area	Surface Area
2	2^3	8 cubic units	2^2	4 square units	6×2^2	24 square units
3						
4						
5						
6						
7						
8						
9						
10						

DO MORE

What patterns or observations do you notice when finding the volume and surface areas of cubes using exponents? Share your thoughts with a partner. Record on the back of this paper.

89

Published by Instructional Fair. Copyright protected.   0-7424-2895-8 *Using the Standards—Measurement*

Name _____ Date _____

Volume and Surface Area Exponents

An exponent is a number that tell how many times the base is used as a factor. Exponents can be used to find the volume and surface area of a cube.

volume: $4 \times 4 \times 4 = 4^3 = 64$ cubic units

area of one side: $4 \times 4 = 4^2 = 16$ square units

surface area: $6 \times$ area of one side $= 6 \times (4 \times 4) = 6 \times 4^2 = 96$ square units

Look at each figure.

    a. Write a multiplication problem to find the volume. Rewrite the problem using an exponent. Remember to label using cubic units.

    b. Write a multiplication problem to find the surface area. Rewrite the problem using an exponent. Remember to label using square units.

1.   volume   _____   _____

     surface area   _____   _____

3 ft.

2.   volume   _____   _____

     surface area   _____   _____

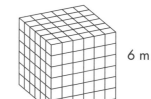

6 m

3.   volume   _____   _____

     surface area   _____   _____

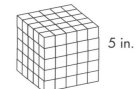

5 in.

4.   volume   _____   _____

     surface area   _____   _____

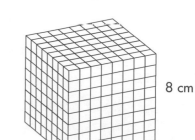

8 cm

0-7424-2895-8 *Using the Standards—Measurement*

Name _____ Date _____

Dunk It

You need a variety of small waterproof objects that sink, a basin or bucket, a milliliter measuring container, water, and centimeter cubes (linking cubes if possible).

List your small waterproof objects in the first column of the table. Use centimeter cubes to estimate the volume of each figure. Write the estimated volume in the table. Measure the actual volume in milliliters. Put water in the measuring container. Write down the amount. Drop in the object. Subtract the amount of water displaced by the object from its original volume.

I cubic centimeter = I milliliter

Object	Estimated Volume in Cubic Centimeters	Actual Measure in Milliliters	Difference from Original Water Level

DO MORE

Explain how you estimated volume using centimeter cubes.

0-7424-2895-8 *Using the Standards—Measurement*

Name _____ Date _____

Pour It In

You will need graduated cylinders of different sizes, six containers to measure volume (remove any labels), and water, rice, or small objects to use to measure.

Choose six containers. Estimate the volume of each in metric units. Then find the actual volume of each. Then estimate and find the actual measurement in customary units. Record the data collected in the table below.

Container	Metric Estimate	Actual Measure	Customary Estimate	Actual Measure
container 1				
container 2				
container 3				
container 4				
container 5				
container 6				

How does the shape of the container affect your ability to estimate volume?

_____

_____

_____

DO MORE

Compare your data with a partner. Develop a more accurate way to estimate volume.

Name _____ Date _____

Six Steps or Less

You will need a pan balance, masses, and objects to measure mass.

Choose an object. Place it in Pan A. Find its mass in 6 steps or less. Record your sequence of tries. Explain each try. For example, did you add mass or take away mass? Why? How did you choose the size of the next mass?

Object 1 _____ Estimated mass _____

Step a: amount on pan B _____ explanation _____

Step b: amount on pan B _____ explanation _____

Step c: amount on pan B _____ explanation _____

Step d: amount on pan B _____ explanation _____

Step e: amount on pan B _____ explanation _____

Step f: amount on pan B _____ explanation _____

Object 2 _____ Estimated mass _____

Step a: amount on pan B _____ explanation _____

Step b: amount on pan B _____ explanation _____

Step c: amount on pan B _____ explanation _____

Step d: amount on pan B _____ explanation _____

Step e: amount on pan B _____ explanation _____

Step f: amount on pan B _____ explanation _____

Object 3 _____ Estimated mass _____

Step a: amount on pan B _____ explanation _____

Step b: amount on pan B _____ explanation _____

Step c: amount on pan B _____ explanation _____

Step d: amount on pan B _____ explanation _____

Step e: amount on pan B _____ explanation _____

Step f: amount on pan B _____ explanation _____

0-7424-2895-8 *Using the Standards—Measurement*

Name _____ Date _____

Around the Room

You will need a pan balance; 1-gram, 5-gram, 20-gram, 50-gram, and 1-kilogram masses; and four objects to measure mass.

You have a pan balance and only one of each of the following masses; 1-gram, 5-gram, 20-gram, 50-gram, and 1-kilogram. Your assignment is to measure the mass of four objects to the nearest gram. None of the four objects can be exactly any one of the given masses or an exact combination of the masses. Find a way to measure the mass of your four objects. You may use any objects available in your classroom except additional masses. Explain your method clearly.

_____

_____

_____

_____

_____

Object 1   estimated mass _____   actual mass _____

Object 2   estimated mass _____   actual mass _____

Object 3   estimated mass _____   actual mass _____

Object 4   estimated mass _____   actual mass _____

DO MORE

Compare your method of measurement with another student.

0-7424-2895-8 *Using the Standards—Measurement*

Name _____ Date _____

Celsius or Fahrenheit

A group of students researched temperature and recorded the following measurements. They forgot to add the units when recording the temperatures. Figure out whether Celsius or Fahrenheit was used. Write *C* for Celsius or *F* for Fahrenheit in the box following the degrees. The teacher wants all temperatures recorded in Celsius. Use the thermometer to help you. Change each Fahrenheit temperature to Celsius and write it on the line.

1. body temperature: 99 degrees ☐ _____

2. room temperature: 20 degrees ☐ _____

3. temperature at the North Pole: 28 degrees ☐ _____

4. temperature at the equator: 30 degrees ☐ _____

5. temperature on a good day to make a snowman: 32 degrees ☐ _____

6. temperature of a mug of hot chocolate: 50 degrees ☐ _____

7. refrigerator temperature (not freezer): 5 degrees ☐ _____

8. hot tub temperature: 102 degrees ☐ _____

9. temperature on a summer day: 35 degrees ☐ _____

C   F

50°   130°
      120°
40°   110°
      100°
30°   90°
      80°
20°   70°
      60°
10°   50°
      40°
0°   30°
      20°
-10°   10°
      0°
-20°   -10°

95

0-7424-2895-8 *Using the Standards—Measurement*

Name _____ Date _____

Ice Water

You will need a thermometer, four glasses of the same size, three larger containers, ice, and hot and cold water. This activity can be completed independently, with partners, or in small groups.

Fill glass 1 with ice then add water.

Fill glass 2 half full of ice then add water to the same level as glass 1.

Fill glass 3 with cold tap water.

Fill glass 4 with hot water.

Feel the water in each glass. Estimate the temperature of each glass of water in both Fahrenheit and Celsius.

Glass 1

estimate _____ °C _____ °F   actual _____ °C _____ °F

Glass 2

estimate _____ °C _____ °F   actual _____ °C _____ °F

Glass 3

estimate _____ °C _____ °F   actual _____ °C _____ °F

Glass 4

estimate _____ °C _____ °F   actual _____ °C _____ °F

Pour glass 1 and glass 2 together. Feel the water. What is your estimate of the temperature?
_____ °C _____ °F

Measure the actual temperature. _____ °C _____ °F

Pour glass 3 and glass 4 together. Feel the water. What is your estimate of the temperature?
_____ °C _____ °F

Measure the actual temperature. _____ °C _____ °F

0-7424-2895-8 *Using the Standards—Measurement*

Name _____ Date _____

Checking Labels

Choose the most sensible measurement.

1.	volume of a soup can	355 milliliters	355 liters	355 kiloliters
2.	length of a calculator	5 inches	5 feet	5 yards
3.	mass of a pencil	3 milligrams	3 kilograms	3 grams
4.	top speed an ostrich can run	40 miles per second	40 miles per minute	40 miles per hour
5.	length a gargoyle extends from a building	3 inches	3 feet	3 miles
6.	volume of a juice pitcher	2 fluid ounces	2 quarts	2 tablespoons
7.	weight of the Statue of Liberty	225 ounces	225 pounds	225 tons
8.	depth of a pond	4 meters	4 centimeters	4 kilometers
9.	weight of a gorilla	450 tons	450 ounces	450 pounds
10.	length of a bee	2.5 millimeters	2.5 centimeters	2.5 meters

DO MORE

What measuring tool would you use to measure each of the items above?

Published by Instructional Fair. Copyright protected.

0-7424-2895-8 *Using the Standards—Measurement*

Name _____ Date _____

Let's Compare

Compare these items. Write **<**, **>**, or **=** between them. Find an appropriate measurement tool for each set of objects.

1. Fresh French fries are _____ a pickle in temperature.
Measurement tool _____

2. The angle of a square window is _____ the angle of a rectangular door.
Measurement tool _____

3. A basketball is _____ a tennis ball in weight/mass.
Measurement tool _____

4. A mug is _____ a tea kettle in volume.
Measurement tool _____

5. Jesse's new yellow #2 pencil is _____ Jacob's new #2 yellow pencil in length.
Measurement tool _____

6. A snowball is _____ a glass of water in temperature.
Measurement tool _____

7. A cereal bowl is _____ a spoon in volume.
Measurement tool _____

8. A watermelon is _____ an orange in weigh/mass.
Measurement tool _____

9. An earthworm is _____ a cobra in length.
Measurement tool _____

10. The angle of two sides meeting on a stop sign is _____ the angle of two sides meeting on a speed limit sign.
Measurement tool _____

DO MORE

Choose three of the above objects. Determine reasonable units and approximate measurements.

0-7424-2895-8 *Using the Standards—Measurement*

Name _____ Date _____

Grab the Right Measuring Tool

Circle the most reasonable measuring tool needed to answer each of the following questions.

1. The knob on the stove is turned to the off position. How far must it be turned for the temperature to be at 350 degrees?

   ruler   protractor   pan balance

2. The carrots purchased at the farmers' market are in a long, thin paper bag. The price is determined by the number of ounces. How much will the carrots cost?

   ruler   scale   thermometer

3. The hexagonal fish tank is the same length as the rectangular tank. How much water will it hold?

   graduated cylinder   pan balance   ruler

4. Is the hot chocolate in the 16-ounce mug cool enough to drink?

   graduated cylinder   pan balance   thermometer

5. How much vinyl trim is needed to edge the bath tub where it meets the floor?

   graduated cylinder   ruler   pan balance

DO MORE

Determine an appropriate measurement for each of the above situations.

0-7424-2895-8 *Using the Standards—Measurement*

Name _____ Date _____

Put Them on the Shelf

Use the clues to put each measuring tool back on the shelf in correct order. The first object is on the left.

1.

The measuring tools used to find volume each have only one neighbor. The tool with a Celsius scale is next to the one that measures in grams. The mass measurer comes after the tool that measures length and is right next to the one that measures milliliters.

_____

_____

_____

_____

_____

2.

The last three items measure standard units. The two objects that measure length have two tools between them. The measuring tool that measures weight is not last. The two that measure volume have two other tools between them. Neither of the items that measure volume are first.

_____

_____

_____

_____

_____

DO MORE

Choose one of the measuring tools. List five items you could measure with it.

100

Name _____ Date _____

What to Do

Read each situation. Then form a plan. Write what you will measure, with what tool, in which kind of units, and an estimated measurement.

1. Mikaela has a bowl of water. She wants to know how much water is in her bowl. Use a metric unit.

    Object _____   Tool   _____
    Unit   _____   Measurement _____

2. Willie is making a picture frame with equal sides. He is attaching the corners and wants to know far apart to spread each of the side pieces.

    Object _____   Tool   _____
    Unit   _____   Measurement _____

3. Abimael picked a bucket of blueberries. He needs to know how heavy the blueberries are so that he can pay for them. Use standard units.

    Object _____   Tool   _____
    Unit   _____   Measurement _____

4. Madalen needs a blanket that will cover the side of her bunk bed to make a tent. She wants to know how long and how wide the blanket needs to be. Use standard units.

    Object _____   Tool   _____
    Unit   _____   Measurement _____

5. Jesse wants to know which block of wood is the heaviest. Use metric units.

    Object _____   Tool   _____
    Unit   _____   Measurement _____

6. Rocio boiled a cup of water. She wants to know if it is cool enough to drink. Use metric units.

    Object _____   Tool   _____
    Unit   _____   Measurement _____

Published by Instructional Fair. Copyright protected.   0-7424-2895-8 *Using the Standards—Measurement*

Name _____ Date _____

Attention All Units

Use the clues and the problem solving matrix to determine who is using each unit of measure.

Brett, Jack, and Loni are using metric measures.

Neither Dena nor Will are measuring volume.

Will and Loni are measuring the same thing, but with different units.

Haley is using quarts to measure the volume of her liquid.

Dena found out her object is exactly 16 ounces.

Jack is not measuring mass.

	Celsius	Centimeters	Fahrenheit	Fluid Ounces	Grams	Quarts	Pounds
Brett							
Dena							
Haly							
Jack							
Kris							
Loni							
Will							

Brett's unit is _____.

Dena's unit is _____.

Haly's unit is _____.

Jack's unit is _____.

Kris's unit is _____.

Loni's unit is _____.

Will's unit is _____.

DO MORE

 Name each student's measuring tool.

Published by Instructional Fair. Copyright protected.

0-7424-2895-8 *Using the Standards—Measurement*

Name _____ Date _____

Estimate and Measure

Choose an object to measure. Record the type of measure and the measurement tool. Estimate the measurement, then record the actual measurement. Do not forget units.

Object: _____   Object: _____

Type of Measure: _____   Type of Measure: _____

Measurement Tool: _____   Measurement Tool: _____

Estimate: _____   Estimate: _____

Actual Measure: _____   Actual Measure: _____

Object: _____   Object: _____

Type of Measure: _____   Type of Measure: _____

Measurement Tool: _____   Measurement Tool: _____

Estimate: _____   Estimate: _____

Actual Measure: _____   Actual Measure: _____

Object: _____   Object: _____

Type of Measure: _____   Type of Measure: _____

Measurement Tool: _____   Measurement Tool: _____

Estimate: _____   Estimate: _____

Actual Measure: _____   Actual Measure: _____

Object: _____   Object: _____

Type of Measure: _____   Type of Measure: _____

Measurement Tool: _____   Measurement Tool: _____

Estimate: _____   Estimate: _____

Actual Measure: _____   Actual Measure: _____

DO MORE

Check actual measures with a partner for accuracy. How do your estimates compare to the actual measures?

0-7424-2895-8 *Using the Standards—Measurement*

Name _____ Date _____

Create Your Own Problems I

1. Design an activity to demonstrate your knowledge of finding estimated area, perimeter, or volume.

2. Draw shapes within a shape using rectangles, parallelograms, and triangles. Find the area of certain parts of the whole.

3. Use a chosen number of cubes. Build a variety of irregular shapes using this volume. Find the surface area of each figure. Remember, each exposed side of a cube must be counted to find the surface area. Check the surface area of each figure with two partners. Any disagreements must result in a recount and check for accuracy. Determine a way to record shapes and their surface areas.

4. Make 5 cards with the volume and surface area for a cube written using exponents. For example: volume = 5^3, surface area = 6×5^2. Write the answers on the back of the card. Trade cards. Build the figures described. Find the volume and surface area of each figure. Check your answers using the back of each card.

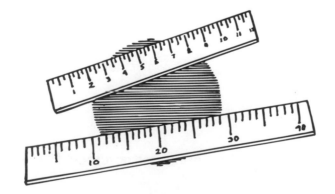

　　　　　0-7424-2895-8 *Using the Standards—Measurement*

Name _____   Date _____

Create Your Own Problems II

1. Design an angle activity that demonstrates your knowledge of angle measures. Include each type of angle and how angle measures relate to each other.

2. Make one list of measurement types, a second list of measurement tools, and a third list of measurement units. Design a game that would cause students to match the cards and then name an object that could be measured in this way.

3. Write your own riddles dealing with measurement. Write the riddle on one side of a 3 x 5 in. card. Write the answer on the back. Combine cards for a class activity.

4. Demonstrate your understanding of precision by making a list of measurement units and situations when it would be the most reasonable unit to use.

5. Design a poster demonstrating your knowledge and understanding of the techniques and tools of measuring. Design an attribute check list for this poster in a small group or as a class. This list should include attributes of quality as well as the number of content items needed.

   0-7424-2895-8 *Using the Standards—Measurement*

Name _____ Date _____

Check Your Skills

Name the tool used to measure and name an appropriate unit to use to answer each of the following questions.

1. How wide is this book?   tool _____ unit _____

2. Is this soup cool enough to eat?   tool _____ unit _____

3. How heavy is this dog?   tool _____ unit _____

Find the estimated area of these shapes.

4.  _____   **5.**  _____

Circle the appropriate unit.

6. The temperature in the classroom is 20 degrees . . .   Celsius   Fahrenheit

7. The volume of a pack of gum is 16 cubic . . .   centimeters   meters

8. The distance from our classroom to the playground is 87 . . .   inches   feet

Measure each angle. Write the name of the angle type.

9. _____

10. _____

11. _____

12. _____

13. _____

Write the measure of each angle.

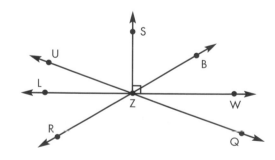

14. ∠BZW _____   **17.** ∠RZL _____   **20.** ∠BZQ _____

15. ∠UZW _____   **18.** ∠RZQ _____   **21.** reflex ∠WZQ _____

16. ∠UZS _____   **19.** ∠QZW _____   **22.** reflex ∠LZB _____

0-7424-2895-8 *Using the Standards—Measurement*

Name _____ Date _____

Check Your Skills (cont.)

Find the area of each part of the figure. Then answer the questions.

23. figure M area _____

24. figure N area _____

25. figure O area _____

26. figure P area _____

27. figure Q area _____

28. figure R area _____

29. figure S area _____

30. figure T area _____

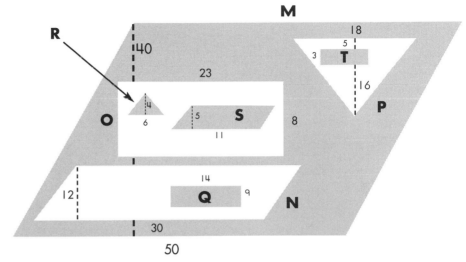

31. What are the perimeters of figures O, Q, and T? O = _____ Q = _____ T = _____

32. What is the area of all the shaded portions inside figure M? _____

33. Make two figures with an area of 9. Each figure must have a different perimeter. Label the perimeter.

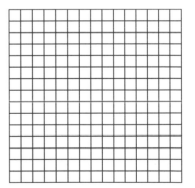

34. Make two figures with a perimeter of 16. Each figure must have a different area. Label the area.

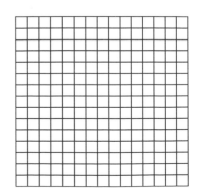

107

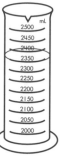

Post Test

Find the measure.

1. _____

2. _____

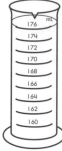

Measure each angle. Identify the type of angle by writing the angle name.

3. _____ _____

4. _____ _____

5. _____ _____

6. _____ _____

7. _____ _____

8.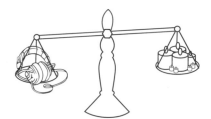

🕯	= 10 grams
🕯	= 5 grams
🕯	= 1 gram

What does this tell you about the mass of the headphones?

_____

9. Meg poured 464 mL of soda into each of 2 glasses from an unopened 2 liter bottle. How much soda is left in the bottle? _____

10. A package weighs 8 pounds. One item in it weighs 52 ounces. How much does the other item(s) weigh? _____

0-7424-2895-8 *Using the Standards—Measurement*

Name _____ Date _____

Post Test (cont.)

Circle each unit used for each type of measure.

11. temperature: Celsius   gram   ounce   Fahrenheit   metric ton

12. length: milligram   decimeter   yard   kilometer   kiloliter

13. volume/capacity: cubic centimeter   milliliter   cubic inch   cubic gram   liter

14. time: gram   second   month   deciliter   Celsius

Find the perimeter.

15. _____

45
32

16. _____

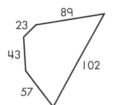
89
23
43
102
57

Find the area for each of these figures.

17. _____

12
13

18. _____

59
76

Measure each angle.

19. ∠KMN _____

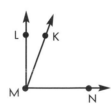
L   K
M   N

20. ∠VQR _____

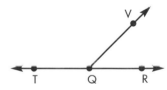
V
T   Q   R

21. Without using a protractor, what is the measure of ∠LMK? _____ ∠TQV? _____

Find the volume and surface area of each figure.

22. volume _____

surface area _____

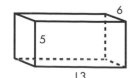
6
5
13

23. volume _____

surface area _____

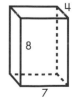
4
8
7

0-7424-2895-8 *Using the Standards—Measurement*

Answer Key

Pretest ....**pages 7–8**

1. Add more mass—2 grams. Current total is 17 grams; 20 was too much; best answer is to add 2 grams.
2. centimeters
3. cubic yards
4. miles
5. grams
6. liters
7. p = 55 units
8. 48 square units
9. 2.156 kilograms
10. acute angle = between 0 and 90 degrees
11. obtuse angle = between 90 and 180 degrees
12. reflex angle = between 180 and 360 degrees
13. right angle = 90 degrees
14. straight angle = 180 degrees
15. 64 ounces
16. 5° C
17. 1.9 m
18. 64 fluid ounces
19. 352 cubic units; 328 square units
20. 3,648 cubic units; 1,448 square units
21. 30 degrees
22. 155 degrees
23. 60 degrees; 25 degrees
24. 2,600 mL
25. 430 mL

Inching Along ....**page 9**

1. $3\frac{1}{2}$ inch line
2. a–c. Accept any reasonable answer.
3. a–c. Accept any reasonable answer.
4. $7\frac{1}{4}$ inch line
5. a–f. Accept any reasonable answer.
6. $5\frac{1}{8}$ inch line
7. a–c. Accept any reasonable answer.
8. a–c. Accept any reasonable answer.

Collecting Centimeters ....**page 10**

1. 12 centimeter line
2. a–c. Accept any reasonable answer.
3. a–c. Accept any reasonable answer.
4. 6 centimeter line
5. a–f. Accept any reasonable answer.
6. 19 centimeter line
7. a–c. Accept any reasonable answer.
8. a–c. Accept any reasonable answer.

Looking for the Best Answer ....**page 11**

1. 18.5 cm
2. 45 mm
3. 2.05 m
4. 6.5 dm
5. 15 cm
6. 28.5 mm
7. 5.8 dm
8. 10.2 mm
9. 40 m
10. 1.4 dm

The Bugs Are Marching ....**pages 12–13**

1. 1 cm; 13 mm; in matrix: 1.3 cm
2. 3 cm; 31 mm; in matrix: 3.1 cm
3. 2 cm; 24 mm; in matrix: 2.4 cm
4. 1 cm; 8 mm; in matrix: 0.8 cm
5. 3 cm; 27 mm; in matrix: 2.7 cm
6. 2 cm; 16 mm; in matrix: 1.6 cm

Blue bug is 5, 2.7 cm.
Green bug is 4, 0.8 cm.
Orange bug is 3, 2.4 cm.
Purple bug is 2, 3.1 cm.
Red bug is 6, 1.6 cm.
Yellow bug is 1, 1.3 cm.
All 6 combined: 11.9 cm

Checking the Line ....**page 14**

1. 2 inches
2. $2\frac{1}{2}$ inches
3. $2\frac{1}{4}$ inches
4. $2\frac{3}{8}$ inches
5. $2\frac{5}{16}$ inches
6. 4 inches
7. 4 inches
8. $3\frac{3}{4}$ inches
9. $3\frac{7}{8}$ inches
10. $3\frac{13}{16}$ inches
11. Answers will vary.
12. Answers will vary.

From Volcanoes to the Ocean ....**page 15**

1. 1 mile = 5,280 feet
   Kilauea is 1,363 yards 1 foot
   Mauna Loa is 2 miles 1,039 yards
2. 1 yard = 36 inches
   porpoise is 2 yards 8 inches
   dolphin is 10 yards
   humpback whale is 20 yards 1 foot 8 inches

Crafters ....**page 16**

1. 356 + 127 + 462 + 198 = 1,143 inches; 1,143 ÷ 12 = 95 feet 3 inches
2. 25 ft. x 12 = 300 inches; 300 ÷ 4 = 75 four-inch pieces
3. $2\frac{1}{2}$ x 7 = $17\frac{1}{2}$ hours; $17\frac{1}{2}$ x 4 = 70 inches; 70 ÷ 12 = 5 feet 10 inches
   1 foot 10 inches on second scarf; still needs 2 feet and 2 inches or 26 inches @ 4 inches in one hour = $6\frac{1}{2}$ hours

0-7424-2895-8 *Using the Standards—Measurement*

Answer Key

Metric Length Conversions
1 m = 1,000 mm
1 m = 100 cm
1 dkm = 1,000 cm
1 dkm = 100 dm
1 hm = 10 dkm
1 km = 100 dkm
1 km = 10 hm

1. meters or decameters; decimeters too short, hectometers too long
2. centimeters or decimeters; millimeters too short, meters too long
3. 15.7 dm, 157 cm, 1.57 meters
4. 489.3 dkm, 4,893 m, 4.893 km
5. 91 mm, 9.1 cm

Around the Room, Metric Length
Table One
1. 600 mm, 60 cm, 6 dm, 0.6 m
2. 23 mm, 2.3 cm, 0.23 dm, 0.023 m
3. 720 mm, 72 cm, 7.2 dm, 0.72 m
4. 540 mm, 54 cm, 5.4 dm, 0.54 m

Longer and Shorter
1. 4 and 5 inch lines
   Answers will vary, but must be accurate.
2. 14 and 15 inch lines
   Answers will vary, but must be accurate.

Can We Agree?
Ranges will vary, but should be within 1–2 mm.
1. 4 mm
2. 2 mm
3. 7 mm
4. 5 mm
5. 11 mm
6. 9 mm
7. 14 mm
8. 11 mm
9. 1 mm
10. 6 mm

Accuracy Counts
Answers will vary, but must be accurate. Ranges will vary.

Checking Angles
1. 180 degrees
2. 90 degrees
3. 360 degrees
4. 270 degrees

acute angle—an angle that measures between 1 and 90 degrees
reflex angle—an angle that measures between 180 and 360 degrees
obtuse angle—an angle that measures between 90 and 180 degrees

Locating the Angles
There are four acute, two right, three obtuse, three straight, and three reflex angles.

Measure the Angles
1. 180 degrees, straight angle
2. 35 degrees, acute angle
3. 106 degrees, obtuse angle
4. 340 degrees, reflex angle
5. 90 degrees, right angle
6. 195 degrees, reflex angle
7. 15 degrees, acute angle
8. 100 degrees, obtuse angle
9. 255 degrees, reflex angle

Scrutinizing Angles
1. 25 degrees
2. 180 degrees
3. 155 degrees
4. 25 degrees
5. 180 degrees
6. 155 degrees
7. 120 degrees
8. 180 degrees
9. 60 degrees
10. 120 degrees
11. 180 degrees
12. 60 degrees
13. 45 degrees
14. 180 degrees
15. 135 degrees
16. 45 degrees
17. 180 degrees
18. 135 degrees
19. Answers will vary.

Angles in Shapes
1. triangle (3-sided figure) with one 60 degree angle; measure of other two angles will vary, but must be accurate
2. quadrilateral (4-sided figure) with one 95 degree angle; measure of other three angles will vary, but must be accurate
3. pentagon (5-sided figure) with one 150 degree angle; measure of other four angles will vary, but must be accurate
4. hexagon (6-sided figure) with one 200 degree angle; measure of other five angles will vary, but must be accurate
5. octagon (8-sided figure) with one 90 degree angle; measure of other seven angles will vary, but must be accurate

Quadrilateral MATH
$\angle MAT = 90°$ Side MA = 2 cm
$\angle ATH = 60°$ Side AT = 5 cm
$\angle THM = 118°$ Side TH = 2.5 cm
$\angle HMA = 90°$ Side HM = 4 cm

0-7424-2895-8 *Using the Standards—Measurement*

Answer Key

Within a Pentagon...**page 28**
1. each angle 108 degrees; sum 540 degrees
2. angle measures are 101, 103, 130, 79, and 127 degrees; sum 540 degrees
3. angle measures are 89, 140, 87, 130, and 94 degrees; sum 540 degrees
4. angle measures are 71, 201, 49, 83, and 136 degrees; sum 540 degrees
5. angle measures are 56, 230, 55, 102, and 97 degrees; sum 540 degrees
6. angle measures are 139, 116, 92, 106, and 87 degrees; sum 540 degrees

Within Shapes ....**page 29**
triangle A—each angle 60 degrees
quadrilateral A—each angle 90 degrees
hexagon A—each angle 120 degrees
octagon A—each angle 135 degrees
nonagon A—each angle 140 degrees
decagon A—each angle 144 degrees
1. all sums 180
2. all sums 360
3. all sums 720
4. all sums 1,080
5. all sums 1,260
6. all sums 1,440

Who Made It? ....**page 30**
figure A: area = 11; perimeter = 16; Tam
figure B: area = 12; perimeter = 16; Val
figure C: area = 12; perimeter = 20; Eli
figure D: area = 9; perimeter = 20; Zoë
figure E: area = 11; perimeter = 20; Abi
figure F: area = 6; perimeter = 14; Kay

Museum Measurement ....**page 31**
1. Sample answers: 2 x 12 figure—28 feet of edging; 3 x 8 figure—22 feet of edging; 4 x 6 figure—20 feet of edging
2. Sample answers: 4 x 16 figure—40 feet of cord; 8 x 8 figure—32 feet of cord; 2 x 32 figure—68 feet of cord
3. Sample answers: 2 x 60 figure—124 feet of filament; 4 x 30 figure—68 feet of filament; 10 x 12 figure—34 feet of filament
4. Sample answers: 7 x 8 figure—30 feet of framing; 1 x 56 figure—114 feet of framing; 4 x 14 figure—36 feet of framing

One Area ....**page 32**
area for each = 10 square units
Perimeters will vary, but must be accurate for figure.

Grid Paper..**page 33**
1. area for each = 15 square units
   Perimeters will vary, but must be accurate for figure
2. area for each = 24 square units
   Perimeters will vary, but must be accurate for figure
3. area for each = 30 square units
   Perimeters will vary, but must be accurate for figure
4. area for each = 36 square units
   Perimeters will vary, but must be accurate for figure

Around the Edge..**page 34**
Some answers will vary.
1. perimeter = 4 units
2. perimeter = 6 units
3. perimeter = 8 units
4. perimeter = 10 units

Perimeter...**page 35**
perimeter = 12; Area and range will vary.
perimeter = 14; Area and range will vary.
perimeter = 16; Area and range will vary.
perimeter = 18; Area and range will vary.
perimeter = 20; Area and range will vary.

Comparing Masses...**page 36**
1. apple—the apple side of the pan balance is lower, which shows it has more mass than the banana.
2. scissors—the marker side of the pan balance is higher, which shows it has less mass than the scissors.
3. Both have the same mass. The two objects balance because they have the same mass.

Determining Masses ....**page 37**
cup down, washer up
Explanation will vary: one washer = 4 grams, one paper clip = 2 grams, 1 cup = 6 grams
Since cup is 6 grams and washer is 4 grams, the cup side has more mass and will be lower.

Next Step ....**page 38**
1. Take mass off pan; 3 grams; Explanation will vary: Pans are nearly balanced, taking 3 grams off is the most reasonable next step.
2. Add more mass; 10 grams; Explanation will vary: Pan A is about halfway between level and its lowest level; 50 is too much; 2 or 1 would probably not be enough; 10 is the best answer.

Fresh Fruit ....**page 39**
apples = 48 ounces; 3 lb.
blueberries = 52 ounces; 3 lb. 4 oz.
bananas = 36 ounces; 2 lb. 4 oz.
peaches = 50 ounces; 3 lb. 2 oz.
plums = 41 ounces, 2 lb. 9 oz.
Order: apples, plums, blueberries, bananas, peaches

Published by Instructional Fair. Copyright protected.

0-7424-2895-8 *Using the Standards—Measurement*

Answer Key

Pounds and Kilograms ....page 40
  1. 94 pounds 4 ounces or 94 $\frac{1}{4}$ pounds
  2. 1,092,870 grams = 1,092.87 kg or 1.09 metric tons
  3. 48 ounces; 44 ounces; 50 ounces
  4. 19 tons 1,897 pounds or about 20 tons
  5. 1,826 kilograms or 1.826 metric tons

Between the Grams ....page 41
Answers will vary, but must be accurate.

Exploring Volume ....page 42
Answers will vary depending on containers. Possible solution would be to pour water or rice from one container to another, using amounts filled to compare.

Varying Volume ....page 43
Correct amount marked on each graduated cylinder.
A = 45 mL
B = 90 mL
C = 30 mL
D = 60 mL
E = 120 mL
F = 15 mL

Finding the Volume of Objects ....page 44
  1. increments: 10 mL; mark at 430 mL; pre-marked: 480 mL; vol. of marble: 50 mL
  2. increments: 1 mL; mark at 72 mL; pre-marked: 79 mL; vol. of thumbtack: 7 mL
  3. increments: 5 mL; mark at 165 mL; pre-marked: 180 mL; vol. of nail: 15 mL

Capacity in the Grocery Aisle ....page 45
Answers in table:
1 cup = 48 teaspoons
1 pint = 16 fluid ounces
1 quart = 4 cups
1 quart = 32 fluid ounces
1 gallon = 16 cups
1 gallon = 8 pints
1 gallon = 4 quarts
1 gallon = 128 fluid ounces

  1. 0.48 ounce or about $\frac{1}{2}$ ounce
  2. 32 quarts; 1,024 ounces; 160 ounces or 5 quarts; canister will last about 6 days
  3. 24 tablespoons; 72 teaspoons; Yes—explanation will vary: 16 oz. = 2 cups. George only needs 1 $\frac{1}{2}$ cups, so a 16-oz. bottle is enough.

Metric Capacity ....page 46
  1. No; 19 liters = 19,000 cubic centimeters, which is not enough space.
  2. 33 milliliters
  3. about 17 tablespoons; about 50 teaspoons
  4. 12 refills
  5. 9 liters; Explanation will vary: 6 kL = 6,000 L, divide this by 500 L = 12 sets of 500 L each that need 3 metric cups, this equals 36 metric cups, divide this by 4, this equals 9 liters of chemicals

Looking at Thermometers ....page 47
Answers are based on readings, not calculations.
  1. 11 degrees C, 52 degrees F
  2. 36 degrees C, 97 degrees F
  3. 53 degrees C, 127 degrees F
  4. -8 degrees C, 19 degrees F

Planning Events ....page 48
Note: If a student has a reasonable explanation for an alternate answer, accept it.
  1. Thursday; Explanations will vary: Mon. and Tues. too cloudy—could snow. Wed. too warm. Thurs. could have frozen ice and no snow.
  2. Friday; Explanations will vary: Sun. cloudy; Thurs. too cold; Sat. too hot; Fri. cool and clear for telescope.
  3. Tuesday; Explanations will vary: cloudy, but still hot and warm water, wouldn't get a sunburn

Celsius and Fahrenheit ....page 49
  1. 77 degrees F   5. 20 degrees C
  2. 131 degrees F   6. 80 degrees C
  3. 50 degrees F   7. 35 degrees C
  4. 23 degrees F   8. 5 degrees C

Wacky Weather ....page 50
  1. 18 degrees F / -8 degrees C
     marked on thermometer at correct temp. -4 degrees C or 25 degrees C
  2. 60 degrees F / 16 degrees C
     marked on thermometer at correct temp. 15 degrees F or -9 degrees C

It's About Time ....page 51
  1. about 922 teeth in a set
     Explanations will vary: 24,000 teeth divided by 52 weeks is about 461 teeth a week. New set is every 2 weeks; 2 x 461 = 922 teeth.
  2. 224 hours in 4 weeks; about 9 days
  3. 4,174 kilometers per week
  4. 56 feet tall; 18 yards 2 feet

0-7424-2895-8 *Using the Standards—Measurement*

Answer Key

As Time Goes By .... page 52

1. 6:38:06, correct time on clock
2. 1:02:21, correct time on clock
3. 4:37:33, correct time on clock
4. 2:21:46, correct time on clock
5. 1:41:46, correct time on clock
6. 4:44:49, correct time on clock

At the Zoo .... page 53

2. 3 yards 6 inches; 8,000 pounds
3. 4 yards; 3,000 pounds
4. 2 yards 2 feet; 2,500 pounds
5. 1 yard 2 feet; 2,750 pounds
6. 5 yards 2 feet; 2,582 pounds
7. 2 yards 3 inches; 450 pounds
8. 2 yards 1 inch; 81 pounds
9. 2 feet 2 inches; 5 pounds 3 ounces
10. 1 yard 2 feet 7 inches; 7,000 pounds
11. 1 yard 1 foot; 600 pounds
12. 3 yards 6 inches; 23 pounds

At the Zoo .... page 54

Neither circle: ostrich, condor
Less than 3 yards only: gorilla, platypus, and wolf
Greater than 500 pounds only: elephant, male walrus, giraffe
Both: white rhinoceros, hippopotamus, female walrus, Galapagos tortoise

Finding the Same Amount .... page 55

1. box around: 18 pints, 8 quarts 4 cups, 34 cups 1 pint
2. triangle around: 14 feet, $4\frac{2}{3}$ yards, 168 inches, 7 feet 84 inches
3. ring around: $3\frac{1}{8}$ pounds, 50 ounces, $2\frac{1}{2}$ pounds 10 ounces
4. star next to: 75 minutes, 69 minutes 360 seconds, 1 hour 11 minutes 240 seconds
5. underline: 13.27 meters, 1,327 centimeters, 0.1327 hectometers, 132.7 decimeters

Ridiculous or Reasonable .... page 56

Reasonable answers given.

1. millimeters
2. tons
3. seconds
4. yards
5. pints
6. milligrams
7. kilometers
8. months
9. grams
10. miles
11. liters
12. kilograms
13. ounces
14. inches

Public Measurement .... page 57

Answers will vary depending on product. Measurements should be accurate.

Check Your Skills .... pages 60–61

1. $3\frac{5}{16}$ inch
2. $2\frac{11}{16}$ inch
3. 52 mm or 5.2 cm
4. 97 mm or 9.7 cm
5. increments: 20 mL; mark at 680 mL; pre-marked at 760 mL; vol. of marble: 80 mL
6. 9 degrees C; 50 degrees F
7. example of an acute angle
8. example of an obtuse angle
9. example of a reflex angle
10. example of a right angle
11. example of a straight angle
12. Answers will vary: The grapes have more mass than the banana.
13. 0.7 cm, 0.07 dm, 0.007 m
14. 3,500 mm, 350 cm, 35 dm
15. 1,440 inches, 120 feet
16. 5 pounds 8 ounces
17. 4,500,000 grams, 4.5 metric tons
18. 256 fluid ounces, 32 cups, 16 pints, 8 quarts
19. 50,000 mL, 0.05 kiloliters
20. 840 hours, 35 days
21. BEC = 180 degrees; AEC = 80 degrees; CED = 100 degrees; DEA = 180 degrees; BED = 80 degrees

Grab a Meter Stick .... page 62

1. 1.8 dm, 18 cm
2. 520 mm, 52 cm
3. 15.1 dm, 151 cm
4. 2.03 m, 203 cm
5. 126 mm, 12.6 cm
6. 2.5 dm, 25 cm

Looking at Length .... page 63

Answers will vary, but must be accurate for objects measured.

114

0-7424-2895-8 *Using the Standards—Measurement*

Answer Key

Angle Work...page 64
1. acute, estimate will vary, 45 degrees
2. obtuse, estimate will vary, 95 degrees
3. reflex, estimate will vary, 215 degrees
4. reflex, estimate will vary, 350 degrees
5. obtuse, estimate will vary, 165 degrees
6. acute, estimate will vary, 20 degrees
7. straight, estimate will vary, 180 degrees
8. reflex, estimate will vary, 300 degrees

The Proper Angle.................................pages 65–66
1. 90 degrees
2. 180 degrees
3. 90 degrees
4. 150 degrees
5. 30 degrees
6. obtuse; it is obviously greater than the 90° angle shown.
7. 30°; it is obviously less than 90°, so it must be 30°.
8. ∠JLA should measure 70°.
9. ∠ZLY is 180°. All straight lines equal 180°.
10. 90 degrees

Estimating Perimeter..................................page 67
Answers will vary.

Comparing Perimeter Estimates......................page 68
Answers will vary. Averages and ranges must be accurate for data collected.

Round and Round.....................................page 69
1. 148 cm
2. 78 inches
3. 133 cm
4. 375 m
5. 64 yd.
6. 996 mm

The Area of a Thing.................................page 70
1. 15 square units
2. 1 full square cut off
   15−1 = 14 square units
3. 9 square units
   between 14 square units and
   9 square units
4. two additional squares
   9 + 2 = 11 square units

Step on It...page 71
Answers will vary. Averages and ranges must be accurate for data collected.

More Things to Step On............................page 72
Answers will vary. Average and range must be accurate for data.

More Things to Measure............................page 73
1. answers may vary slightly: between 36 square units and 48 square units; 36 + 7 = 43 square units
2. answers may vary slightly: between 31 square units and 54 square units; 31 + 7 = 38 square units

Looking at the Whole................................page 74
1. 64 cubic cm
2. 125 cubic cm
3–4. Answers will vary.

Area Exponent.......................................page 75
1. $7 \times 7 = 49$ square ft.; $7^2 = 49$ square ft.
2. $4 \times 4 = 16$ square m; $4^2 = 16$ square m
3. $9 \times 9 = 81$ square in.; $9^2 = 81$ square in.
4. $5 \times 5 = 25$ square yd.; $5^2 = 25$ square yd.
5. $11 \times 11 = 121$ square mm; $11^2 = 121$ square mm
6. $15 \times 15 = 225$ square dm; $15^2 = 225$ square dm

Exploring Rectangular Area.........................page 76
1. l = 6, h = 3, 18 square units
2. l = 3, h = 2, 6 square units
3. l = 4, h = 4, 16 square units
4. l = 7, h = 1, 7 square units
5. l = 3, h = 5, 15 square units
6. l = 9, h = 4, 36 square units
7. l = 5, h = 2, 10 square units
8. l = 4, h = 6, 24 square units

More Rectangles.....................................page 77
1. 2,528 square units
2. 1,272 square units
3. 6,834 square units
4. 11,613 square units
5. 13,468 square units
6. 38,420 square units

Exploring the Area of Parallelograms.............page 78
1. 7 square units
2. 4 square units
3. 12 square units
4. 8 square units
5. 8 square units
6. They have the same area.
7. It makes a rectangle.
8. Length and base are essentially the same measurement.

Rectangles and Parallelograms......................page 79
1. 1,092 square units
2. 1,122 square units
3. 5,152 square units
4. 2,236 square units
5. 2,106 square units
6. 3,216 square units

Published by Instructional Fair. Copyright protected.   0-7424-2895-8 *Using the Standards—Measurement*

Answer Key

Shadows Within Shadows ....page 80
1. 12,348 square units
2. B = 987 square units, C = 208 square units, D = 529 square units, E = 105 square units, F = 1,600 square units, G = 256 square units
3. 11,361 square units
4. 3,116 square units
5. 569 square units

Irregular Towers ....page 81
A. volume = 16 cubic units; surface area = 52 square units
B. volume = 32 cubic units; surface area = 83 square units
C. volume = 40 cubic units; surface area = 58 square units

Building Towers...............................page 82
Volume of Tower: 9, 18, 27, 36, 45, 54, 63, 72
Surface Area of Tower: 30, 42, 54, 66, 78, 90, 102, 114
Patterns could include: volume increases by multiples of 9, surface area increases by 12

Covering Cubes ....page 83
1. a. 27 cubes
   b. 3 centimeters, 9 square centimeters
   c. 3 centimeters, 3 centimeters, 6 squares
   d. 9 square centimeters written in each square
   e. 9 + 9 + 9 + 9 + 9 + 9 = 54 square centimeters
   f. 6 x 9 = 54 square centimeters
2. SA = $6s^2$

Covering Boxes ....page 84
Figure A
length = 6, width = 5, height = 3
side A = 18 square units
side B = 18 square units
side C = 15 square units
side D = 15 square units
side E = 30 square units
side F = 30 square units
Total surface area = 126 square units

Figure B
length = 3, width = 7, height = 4
side A = 12 square units
side B = 12 square units
side C = 28 square units
side D = 28 square units
side E = 21 square units
side F = 21 square units
Total surface area = 122 square units

Figure C
length = 8, width = 2, height = 4
side A = 32 square units
side B = 32 square units
side C = 8 square units
side D = 8 square units
side E = 16 square units
side F = 16 square units
Total surface area = 112 square units

Answers will vary: 2(l x w) + 2 (l x h) + 2 (w x h) = total surface area

Filling Cubes ....page 85
1. b. 16 cubes
   c. 4 layers
   d. 64 cubes, volume
2. equation: s x s x s = c
3. 16 square centimeters, 96 square units

 0-7424-2895-8 *Using the Standards—Measurement*

Answer Key

Filling More Boxes..................................page 86
1. 6 cubes
2. 2 cubes high, 6 cubes in layer, 12 cubes in all
3. 12 cubes
4. 12 cubes, 24 cubes total
5. 3 cubes high, 12 cubes in layer, 36 cubes in all

Figure A: length = 3, width = 2, height = 2, volume = 12 cubic units

Figure B: length = 4, width = 3, height = 3, volume = 36 cubic units

Figure C: volume = 30 cubic units

Figure D: volume = 48 cubic units

6. The length times the width times the height (the three dimensions of a prism) equal the volume.
7. Volume is the space inside a figure. The space has three dimensions, so a unit that also has three dimensions (a cube) is an appropriate measure. Also, a cube is the same size in all dimensions so it is easy to use to measure.

Centimeter Cube Figures ....page 87
1. volume = 8 cm^3, surface area = 24 cm^2
2. volume = 30 cm^3, surface area = 62 cm^2
3. volume = 40 cm^3, surface area = 76 cm^2
4. width = 3 cm, surface area = 92 cm^2
5. length = 3 cm, surface area 102 cm^2
6. height = 7 cm, surface area = 64 cm^2
7. answers will vary, length = 2 cm, width = 3 cm, height = 4 cm, surface area = 52 cm^2
8. answers will vary, length = 2 cm, width = 4 cm, height = 6 cm, volume = 48 cm^3

Riddles ....page 88
Answers will vary; one example given for each.
1. length 2 units, width 3 units, height 4 units, surface area 52 square units
2. length 4 units, width 5 units, height 6 units, surface area 148 square units
3. length 4 units, width 4 units, height 4 units, surface area 96 square units
4. length 2 units, width 1 unit, height 43 units, surface area 262 square units

Volume and Surface Area Exponents Table.....page 89
3. 3^3, 27 cubic units, 3^2, 9 square units, 6×3^2, 54 square units
4. 4^3, 64 cubic units, 4^2, 16 square units, 6×4^2, 96 square units
5. 5^3, 125 cubic units, 5^2, 25 square units, 6×5^2, 150 square units
6. 6^3, 216 cubic units, 6^2, 36 square units, 6×6^2, 216 square units
7. 7^3, 343 cubic units, 7^2, 49 square units, 6×7^2, 294 square units
8. 8^3, 512 cubic units, 8^2, 64 square units, 6×8^2, 384 square units
9. 9^3, 729 cubic units, 9^2, 81 square units, 6×9^2, 486 square units
10. 10^3, 1,000 cubic units, 10^2, 100 square units, 6×10^2, 600 square units

Volume and Surface Area Exponents.............page 90
1. $3 \times 3 \times 3 = 27$ cubic ft., $3^3 = 27$ cubic feet; $6(3 \times 3) = 54$ square ft., $6 \times 3^2 = 54$ square ft.
2. $6 \times 6 \times 6 = 216$ cubic m, $6^3 = 216$ cubic m; $6(6 \times 6) = 216$ square m, $6 \times 6^2 = 216$ square m
3. $5 \times 5 \times 5 = 125$ cubic in., $5^3 = 125$ cubic in.; $6(5 \times 5) = 150$ square in., $6 \times 5^2 = 150$ square in.
4. $8 \times 8 \times 8 = 512$ cubic cm, $8^3 = 512$ cubic cm; $6(8 \times 8) = 384$ square cm, $6 \times 8^2 = 384$ square cm

Dunk It...page 91
Answers will vary. Milliliter measures should be accurate for object. Differences accurate for data collected.

Pour It In..page 92
Answers will vary, but should be accurate for objects measured.

Six Steps or Less....................................page 93
Answers will vary. As the student progresses, should make more sense mathematically. For example, if pan B is up, more mass should be added with the amount dependent upon its level compared to pan A. If pan B is down, mass should be eliminated with the amount dependent upon its level compared to pan A.

Around the Room ....page 94
Answers will vary. Will probably include finding objects that do measure 1 gram, 5 grams, etc. to use in place of additional masses. Possibilities also include cups or containers with water, sand, or rice.

0-7424-2895-8 *Using the Standards—Measurement*

Answer Key

Celsius or Fahrenheit ....**page 95**
1. Fahrenheit, 37 degrees C
2. Celsius, 68 degrees F
3. Fahrenheit, -2 degrees C
4. Celsius, 86 degrees F
5. Fahrenheit, 0 degrees C
6. Celsius, 122 degrees F
7. Celsius, 41 degrees F
8. Fahrenheit, 39 degrees C
9. Celsius, 95 degrees F

Ice Water ....**page 96**
Answers will vary, but should be accurate for objects measured.

Checking Labels ....**page 97**
1. 355 milliliters
2. 5 inches
3. 3 grams
4. 40 miles per hour
5. 3 feet
6. 2 quarts
7. 225 tons
8. 4 meters
9. 450 pounds
10. 2.5 centimeters

Let's Compare ....**page 98**
1. >, thermometer
2. =, protractor
3. >, pan balance or scale
4. <, graduated cylinder or measuring cup
5. =, ruler
6. <, thermometer
7. >, graduated cylinder, measuring spoon, or cups
8. >, pan balance or scale
9. <, ruler or measuring tape
10. >, protractor

Grab the Right Measuring Tool ....**page 99**
1. protractor
2. scale
3. graduated cylinder
4. thermometer
5. ruler

Put Them on the Shelf ....**page 100**
1. measuring cup, centimeter ruler, thermometer, pan balance, graduated cylinder
2. centimeter ruler, graduated cylinder, kitchen scale, inch ruler, measuring cup

What to Do ....**page 101**
Note: All reasonable measures will vary.
1. measuring: volume or capacity
   tool: graduated cylinder
   unit of measure: milliliters
   reasonable measure: 850 mL
2. measuring: angles
   tool: protractor
   unit of measure: degrees
   reasonable measure: 90 degrees
3. measuring: weight
   tool: scale
   unit of measure: pounds or ounces
   reasonable measure: 8 pounds
4. measuring: length
   tool: ruler or tape measure
   unit of measure: inches or feet
   reasonable measure: 4 feet by 5 feet
5. measuring: mass
   tool: pan balance
   unit of measure: grams
   reasonable measure: 78 g
6. measuring: temperature
   tool: thermometer
   unit of measure: Celsius
   reasonable measure: 40 degrees Celsius

Attention All Units ....**page 102**
Bret's unit is grams.
Dena's unit is pounds.
Haly's unit is quarts.
Jack's unit is centimeters.
Kris's unit is fluid ounces.
Loni's unit is Celsius.
Will's unit is Fahrenheit.

Estimate and Measure ....**page 103**
Answers will vary. Measurement tools must match type of measure, and labels must be reasonable.

0-7424-2895-8 *Using the Standards—Measurement*

Answer Key

1. ruler; inches or centimeters
2. thermometer, Celsius or Fahrenheit
3. scale or balance scale, pounds or kilograms
4. 17 square units
5. 22 square units
6. Celsius
7. centimeters
8. feet
9. 90 degrees, right angle
10. 30 degrees, acute angle
11. 250 degrees, reflex angle
12. 180 degrees, straight angle
13. 105 degrees, obtuse angle
14. 31 degrees
15. 160 degrees
16. 70 degrees
17. 31 degrees
18. 130 degrees
19. 20 degrees
20. 51 degrees
21. 340 degrees
22. 211 degrees
23. 2,000 square units
24. 360 square units
25. 184 square units
26. 144 square units
27. 126 square units
28. 12 square units
29. 55 square units
30. 15 square units
31. O = 62 units, Q = 46 units, T = 16 units
32. 208 square units
33. perimeters will vary, but must be accurate; all figures with area of 9
34. areas will vary, but must be accurate; all figures with perimeter of 16

1. 2,350 mL
2. 176 mL
3. 140 degrees, obtuse angle
4. 310 degrees, reflex angle
5. 60 degrees, acute angle
6. 180 degrees, straight angle
7. 90 degrees, right angle
8. The object's mass is greater than 39 grams; add mass to pan to make them level.
9. 1,536 mL or 1.536 L
10. 76 ounces or $4\frac{3}{4}$ pounds
11. Celsius, Fahrenheit
12. decimeter, yard, kilometer
13. cubic centimeter, milliliter, cubic inch, liter
14. second, month
15. 154 units
16. 314 units
17. 78 square units
18. 4,484 square units
19. 70 degrees
20. 45 degrees
21. 20 degrees; 135 degrees
22. 390 cubic units; 346 square units
23. 224 cubic units; 232 square units

 0-7424-2895-8 *Using the Standards—Measurement*

Reproducible Rulers

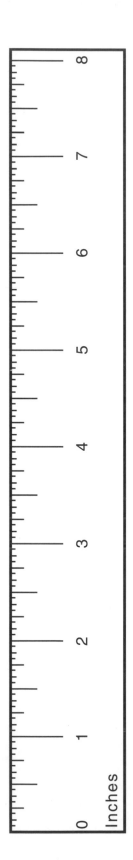

0-7424-2895-8 *Using the Standards—Measurement*

customary system

metric system

volume

capacity

temperature

length

Published by Instructional Fair. Copyright protected.

0-7424-2895-8 *Using the Standards—Measurement*

measuring system used world-wide except in the United States, where it is generally used in scientific study; the modern system is called the International System of Units (SI)

measuring system generally used to measure everyday objects in the United States; also called standard system or English system

measure of the amount something can hold

measure of space inside a solid figure, labeled in cubic units

measure of distance

measure of the amount of heat or cold

0-7424-2895-8 *Using the Standards—Measurement*

mass	**weight**
Celsius	**Fahrenheit**
gram	**meter**

0-7424-2895-8 *Using the Standards—Measurement*

measure of the amount based on gravity

measure of the amount of matter present

unit of measure used for measuring temperature with a Fahrenheit thermometer

freezing point = 32 degrees
boiling point = 212 degrees

unit of measure used for measuring temperature with a centigrade thermometer

freezing point = 0 degrees
boiling point = 100 degrees

the basic unit for measuring length in the metric system

1 meter = 1,000 millimeters, 100 centimeters, or 10 decimeters
1,000 meters = 1 kilometer

the basic unit for measuring mass in the metric system

1000 grams = 1 kilogram
1,000 kilograms = 1 metric ton

0-7424-2895-8 *Using the Standards—Measurement*

pound	**liter**
foot	**cup**
area	**perimeter**

0-7424-2895-8 *Using the Standards—Measurement*

basic unit used to measure
capacity in the metric system

1,000 milliliters = 1 liter
1,000 liters = 1 kiloliter

unit of measure used to
measure weight in the
customary system

16 ounces = 1 pound
2,000 pounds = 1 ton

unit used to measure capacity
in the customary system

1 cup = 8 fluid ounces or
16 tablespoons
2 cups = 1 pint
2 pints = 1 quart
4 quarts = 1 gallon

unit used to measure
length in the customary
system

1 foot = 12 inches
3 feet = 1 yard
1 mile = 1,760 yards

linear measure of an
outer boundary of an area
or shape

measure of a surface,
labeled in square units

0-7424-2895-8 *Using the Standards—Measurement*

surface area

acute angle

right angle

obtuse angle

straight angle

reflex angle

0-7424-2895-8 *Using the Standards—Measurement*

angle with a measure between 0 and 90 degrees

total area measure of each surface of a solid

angle with a measure between 90 and 180 degrees

angle with a measure of 90 degrees

angle with a measure between 180 and 360 degrees

angle with a measure of 180 degrees (a straight line)

0-7424-2895-8 *Using the Standards—Measurement*